INCREDIBLY
DECADENT
DESSERTS

INCREDIBLY
DECADENT
DESSERTS

DEB WISE

**Over 100 Divine Treats
with 300 Calories or Less**

Oxmoor
House®

MY METHODS

I have a dream job. I spend my days thinking up ideas for desserts, and then I make and test them. The initial spark of an idea might start with a memory or be inspired by something I recently tasted or read about. It's typical for me to go through a few iterations to get the dessert just right and make sure it meets *Cooking Light*'s nutritional standards. My challenge is always to produce the same gratifying desserts you would enjoy in a bakery or a restaurant, just in a package that's 300 calories or less. Then the magazine staff tastes it and decides if it rates high enough to be published. Fortunately, this type of tinkering—using ingredients smartly, adjusting baking times to get the perfect texture and browning, and playing with other elements to create the perfect dessert—is why I love what I do.

When developing a new light dessert, I have a few tricks up my sleeve. I manage the sugar content by using assertive ingredients to wring out absolutely every bit of flavor, like high-quality vanilla extract, lemon rind, and almond paste. I use the freshest fruit at the peak of its season. I put just a dash of salt in everything, even in an eggy custard, to balance it and bring out flavors.

Saturated fat is the most difficult part to get right in any light dessert. Dessert needs the richness added by fat to have the right mouthfeel—whether it's moist and cakey, or creamy, or crisp, or flaky like a piecrust. Truthfully, piecrust is one of the hardest things to make light because butter is the key to those wonderful layers. Often I substitute canola oil or egg white for some of the butter, and I've also started using non-hydrogenated natural shortening to get those flaky layers. (It took me a long time to convince *Cooking Light*'s dietitian to sanction it.) I also discovered that adding vinegar and baking powder helps create the right texture. And in other desserts, I like using nut flours because they deliver huge flavor without adding too much fat.

Healthier chocolate desserts are always a challenge. Chocolate itself is high in saturated fat, even though it's plant-based. So I find the richest, deepest chocolate and use it in smaller amounts to keep the flavor as intense as possible. Wait until you taste the Baked Chocolate Mousse (page 233), Mexican Chocolate Cream Pie (page 90), and Seriously Chocolate Cupcakes (page 57). One taste of these rich desserts will have you wondering how they can really be light.

One of my favorite ingredients for keeping light desserts creamy and fluffy is frozen whipped topping. One day I'll write a book called *In Defense of Frozen Reduced-Calorie Whipped Topping,* but for now, you can read a little more about my view on it on page 15. Let's just say, without it, I'd be sunk.

With the resurgence of interest in ancient grains, I wanted to create recipes that included some of them, such as amaranth, teff, and Kamut flours. What I learned through developing these recipes is that you can't just substitute equal amounts of them for regular all-purpose flour. The gluten content in each is different and the flavors are bold. It took me several tries, for example, to get the Cinnamon-Honey Crackers on page 138 just right because the flavor of amaranth is so strong and earthy that it needed to be balanced with just the right amount of all-purpose flour. In the end, I found a happy ratio. You'll find all the desserts that include whole and ancient grains are tagged throughout the book.

A FEW NOTES ON THE RECIPES

You'll find modern recipes, some favorite old-fashioned ones, and a few restaurant-ish desserts like smoked cherry bombs, soufflés, and towering cakes with multiple components. I had so much fun throwing in a few flavor twists on classic desserts, like cardamom in a strawberry-rhubarb pie, a cream pie flavored with chai, and star anise snickerdoodles. I wanted to give you a range of flavors and textures to enjoy.

ADDITIONALLY, YOU CAN EXPECT THAT:

- Some of the recipes may look long or complicated, but the majority are easy.
- A few do take more time but the instructions are clearly written and you will feel confident preparing and serving them.
- Each dessert features the attributes you love in desserts. They are never gummy, dry, or lacking in taste just because they have fewer calories and less fat.
- These recipes do not assume you are an experienced cook.

WHAT YOU'LL LEARN

The most important skill I learned in culinary school was patience. Desserts take time, consideration, and attention. When you're cooking you can make corrections along the way to many dishes when they go wrong, but that's not often true with dessert. With baked treats, you don't know what you're going to get until it comes out of the oven, and sometimes not until you bite into it. And often you're baking for a special occasion and there's no time for a do-over. But there's no need to feel nervous. I've got your back, and you can trust my recipes. Here's my advice: Make a dessert on a day when you have time. If it's for an event, it's often fine to start the day before. Put on music you love, and make sure everybody else in the house is busy and won't interrupt you. There's nothing worse than having to leave the stove while your caramel bubbles or abandon the mixer only to return to deflated egg whites.

Read each recipe all the way through, and prepare all the ingredients before you start mixing. If you're a novice baker, start with something easy, like a Bundt cake (try the one on page 32). Once you've mastered that, move on to a layer cake, and then increase your confidence by preparing a dessert with more components, like a filling or icing (like the cake on page 226). When you feel like trying something new, you may not know all the techniques I've included, but there's nothing to worry about. I've written the instructions clearly to help you power through the critical moments, like how to add a hot simple syrup into whipping egg whites for creamy Italian meringue icing.

Over time, I've learned to be more confident in the kitchen, and you'll get there, too. Be neat and organized and locate all your ingredients and equipment before starting. I get loads of pleasure from the process itself, not just the end result. I'm mesmerized by the texture and color changes that take place during the mixing, folding, stirring, whipping, creaming, and baking steps of a recipe. I hope you learn to love the process, too.

Besides, I've already made all the mistakes so you won't have to. I've made all the desserts multiple times, fixing what turned out to be overly sweet, too dry, too wet, overcooked, undercooked, or flavors that were too harsh or not strong enough. I want every cake, cookie, cobbler, frozen dessert, pie, and pudding to have a wow factor worth your investment of time and energy.

ENJOY THE END RESULT

Our bodies love sugar. I think that's why people get so excited when I bring out a cake or a frozen dessert. Some can hardly wait for the rice pudding to cool enough so they can eat it without burning their tongues. That's why one of the best parts of making a dessert is visualizing the gorgeous end result and anticipating the pleasure that will happen when people taste your masterpiece. It's *so* gratifying.

Good desserts conjure good times and celebrations, like a birthday or a holiday. It's not only the taste but the memories that are integral to our appreciation. So go ahead and show off. People love to celebrate and socialize, and the best fellowship occurs when sharing a meal. These recipes are meant for those occasions. They're indulgent and give you a full blast of flavor and satisfaction, but a lovely little bonus is that they will help you manage calories. You can feel good about sharing them, making them for yourself, and serving them to family and friends.

THE
BASICS

THE BASICS OF LIGHT DESSERTS

I spend so much time making desserts in *Cooking Light*'s Test Kitchen and have gained so much knowledge about ingredients and tools that I want to share all of it with new and experienced bakers. Throughout the book I include details about how ingredients work and why, my top baking tips, and which tools I can't live without. I want you to feel comfortable and confident about making the recipes in *Incredibly Decadent Desserts*. If I succeed, you'll have a trusted collection of desserts that will last for years.

THE BUILDING BLOCKS

Desserts are a combination of art and science. We eat with our eyes first, so desserts simply must look irresistible. If a cake falls or cookies look burned around the edges, the implication is that they won't taste good. You certainly don't want that. And science, the other building block, applies because if you don't follow the recipe, even the finest ingredients will produce a poor dessert. Here are the most critical components and the role they play in taste and texture:

FAT: Butter produces an unrivaled rich flavor in desserts. Since it's high in saturated fat, I use less than in traditional recipes. I don't cut it out altogether because I still want the flavor. Plus, butter plays a crucial role by incorporating air in the creaming process. Aerating butter and sugar by beating them together creates just the right texture that aids leavening. To make up for less butter, I frequently add canola oil, which has the least amount of saturated fat of all oils.

I also substitute egg whites for yolks to cut saturated fat and act as a binder in cakes and doughs. But I don't eliminate all of the egg yolks from a recipe, because the fat in yolks adds tenderness, creaminess, and moisture.

ALL-PURPOSE FLOUR: Flour adds structure to baked goods by building a network of gluten strands that hold in the gas produced during baking and when doughs rise. It thickens pastry cream and pie fillings, and it adds subtle flavor to baked goods, whether you're using a wheat flour or a super-flavorful ancient grain flour. (See page 20 for more whole-grain and nut flours.)

SUGAR: Lighter desserts contain less sugar, period. But in addition to adding sweetness, sugar acts as a preservative in baked goods by adding moisture and by attracting moisture from the environment. Because lighter baked desserts contain less sugar, they have a shorter shelf-life than commercially produced cakes, cookies, and pies. Cold desserts that are naturally stored in the refrigerator (such as cheesecake) will last longer.

SALT: Unless otherwise specified, I use regular table salt—not coarse ground salt or coarse kosher salt. Although my recipes may use less salt than others, I've added enough to bring out the sweetness of fruit and to make cakes and cookies tastier.

IN DEFENSE OF COOL WHIP

I'm a HUGE proponent of real and all-natural flavor additions and ingredients, but when making light desserts, I would be sunk if I didn't have reduced-calorie Cool Whip in my arsenal of tricks. Heavy cream is high in saturated fat and has loads of calories, and you have to use a lot of it to make enough whipped cream to fold into batters or to top pies and cakes. This is where reduced-calorie Cool Whip comes in. Without it, there wouldn't be lighter versions of chocolate mousse cake, dreamy cream pies, or lovely melting dollops on top of warm fruit pies. Every set of rules has an exception, and this is an exception to my rule about only using real ingredients. If you are completely opposed to using whipped topping, here are the substitution facts: 2 tablespoons of reduced-calorie whipped topping contain 25 calories and 1 gram of saturated fat. Substitute an equal amount of heavy cream or whipping cream, and you get 52 calories and 3.5 grams of saturated fat. The difference in saturated fat and calories can really make or break a light dessert. And the texture and flavor are actually so similar, you won't be able to tell the difference.

MY TOP 5
BAKING TIPS

A friend told me once that spending time in my kitchen was a Zen experience. I take that as a compliment. Baking is an art, and you cannot rush and expect to get exceptional results. By incorporating the tips below into your kitchen habits, I hope you, too, will experience the Zen of making desserts.

1 *Read the recipe all the way through, and make sure you have everything you need. A little effort and planning up front could save loads of aggravation down the line. The last thing you need is to discover you're out of sugar in the middle of making cookie dough. So gather all the ingredients, equipment, and tools; chop, toast, and cool nuts and nut flours; make fillings that need to chill; and remember to preheat your oven.*

2 *It's crucial to be mindful of temperature. Always bake desserts at the temperature specified, or they might not rise or set properly. To check that your oven is accurate, or to find hot spots, place an oven thermometer in a few different locations—in the front, in the back, on the sides, and in the lower one-third—to discover if your oven's temperature is consistent throughout. If your oven runs a little hot, check your baked goods early for doneness and vice versa.*

The temperature of your ingredients can make or break your recipe. Pie dough begs for cold butter, but room temperature butter is right for creaming sugar and incorporating air. Follow the guidelines in each recipe. If your butter's too soft, your cookies will be greasy and the size of a dinner plate, your cake will be a gummy mess, and you won't be able to cut your piecrust with a fork. Take butter out of the fridge or freezer in time to have it come to room temperature.

3 *Measure flour accurately. In every recipe that calls for flour, you'll see both a weight as well as a cup measure. The weight measurement is a surefire way to ensure you get the same results I did. The reason is this: Some people pack the flour into measuring cups while others sprinkle it in, and before you know it there might be several ounces too much or too little in the cup. Too much flour could mean your dessert turns out to be dense, heavy, dry, or flat. If you don't own a kitchen scale, I highly recommend that you get one. Then there's no second-guessing yourself, and you'll measure it perfectly every time. If you don't have a scale, follow this scooping advice: Scoop the flour into the cup with a large spoon without packing it in. Level the top with the flat side of a knife.*

4 Be sure to have baking spray with flour on hand. It's awesome. Cakes fall out of their pans with ease, and baking spray with flour won't leave residual white dust on your chocolate cake. Sometimes a warm cake on a cooling rack will stick and tear and leave some of the cake behind. If you spray your rack first, cakes and moist cookies stay beautifully whole. Spray your pans over the open door of your dishwasher to keep overspray mess contained.

5 Use natural flavorings whenever possible. If you're putting all this energy and time into making a dessert, you want it to taste fantastic. The best way to get there is to use real ingredients. (See my exception to this rule on page 15.) Stay away from artificial ingredients concocted in a lab. Artificial flavors contain high amounts of alcohol, coloring agents, artificial sweeteners, and other mysterious ingredients. Use only real vanilla extract, not artificial or vanilla flavoring. Did you know that artificial vanilla has only one or two flavor notes, but real vanilla has hundreds? Isn't that worth paying a little extra?

High-quality liqueurs pack a punch of flavor because they are made from real ingredients that have been distilled in alcohol. A tablespoon or so of Grand Marnier gives you off-the-wall orange flavor, just as a quality amaretto punches up almond flavor. Most of the alcohol burns off during cooking or baking, so you're not left with a dessert that tastes like a cocktail.

BASIC INGREDIENTS

Fresh ingredients are a critical part of any recipe. Check the dates on baking powder and baking soda, and give your canola oil a sniff; if it smells too strong or sour, replace it. If your spices and dried herbs have been in your cupboard so long you can't remember when you bought them, it's time to buy new ones. Flours can be stored in the fridge or freezer, as long as you bring them to room temperature before adding to a recipe. If you don't bake regularly, check the quality of your flour. It might start to smell musty or like the inside of your fridge or freezer. In the cupboard it might go rancid or smell off. Even worse, it might have uninvited residents.

UNBLEACHED ALL-PURPOSE FLOUR: A blend of hard and soft wheat, this flour contains 10 to 13 percent protein. (The higher the protein, the stronger the gluten; bread needs strong gluten, whereas cakes do not.) I recommend unbleached flour to avoid the chemicals used to bleach the flour. Bleached flour has stronger gluten, but doesn't provide enough of a boost to warrant using it.

SEMOLINA FLOUR: Milled from sunny yellow durum wheat, semolina flour has a stronger wheaty flavor and more texture than regular all-purpose flour. Typically it is used to make pasta and pizza dough. In cakes, it adds texture, beautiful golden color, and an enhanced wheat flavor.

CAKE FLOUR: This is soft wheat flour, finely milled, with 7 to 9 percent protein, so there's less strength in the gluten. Use cake flour when you want the softest and most tender cakes.

SUGAR: Buy good-quality sugar cane or sugar beet granulated sugar. If you buy an off brand you've never heard of, it might not be carefully milled. In that case, stubborn organic material can cling to sugar cane and sugar beet crystals during processing, which results in yellowish simple syrups and excess scum floating to the surface of sugar and water boiled for Italian meringues.

BROWN SUGAR: Brown sugar is granulated sugar with molasses added back in. Light brown sugar has about 3.5% molasses, while dark brown sugar has about 6.5%, giving it a richer flavor and deeper color. Brown sugar adds moisture and sweetness to baked goods.

COCOA: Unsweetened cocoa powder is made from roasted, ground cocoa beans that have had most of the cocoa butter removed. Depending on the brand of cocoa, as much as 26% of the cocoa butter can remain in the powder. Natural cocoa powder is acidic and will react with baking soda to get the leavening process in motion. Dutch processed is made from cocoa beans that have been treated with an alkalized solution. You'll get a deeper color and a great chocolaty flavor, but more importantly, the process of Dutching the chocolate renders the powder neutral. If it's used, you will need to kickstart the baking soda with an acidic ingredient, like buttermilk. So be cautious when substituting Dutch processed cocoa for regular cocoa, because you may not get the rise you want and adding too much may have a strange and unappetizing affect on the color.

CORN SYRUP: Some of my recipes include both granulated sugar and corn syrup. While this may seem excessive or redundant, adding corn syrup will prevent crystallization in sugar sauces, such as butterscotch sauce, and make softer and smaller ice crystals in ice creams and sorbets. The corn syrup I use, sold in a bottle in grocery stores, is simply the sugar from the corn, and not high fructose corn syrup.

UNSALTED BUTTER: Unsalted butter allows you to add just enough salt to make the dessert sing. Use the best quality butter you can afford. Cheaper butters often contain more water and less butterfat, reducing the flavor butter brings to baked treats.

NATURAL SHORTENING STICKS: I got so happy when I discovered this alternative to hydrogenated vegetable shortening. Refrigerated natural shortening (such as Earth Balance) has one-third less saturated fat than butter and no unhealthy hydrogenated oils. Combining this shortening with butter makes flaky and tender piecrust. See page 78.

MILK: I'm not partial to any one type of milk. I've specified whole milk, reduced-fat, and fat-free milk throughout this book. In some cases, whole milk will give the finished dessert a richer texture with little additional fat. If you only have fat-free milk on hand, use it. Otherwise, enjoy the extra bit of tenderness and richness in baked goods and ice creams that whole milk provides.

HEAVY CREAM AND HALF-AND-HALF: Whenever possible, a tiny bit of heavy cream or half-and-half will make custards and ice creams so much richer. It doesn't take much to mimic the texture and mouthfeel of full-fat desserts, so don't be afraid to use it in small amounts.

CREAM CHEESE: I'm not a fan of fat-free cream cheese, but when blended with ⅓-less-fat cream cheese, the combination creates richness without extra fat, especially in cheesecakes.

WHOLE-GRAIN AND NUT FLOURS

When incorporating whole grains into your desserts, it's important to know that they can't be swapped cup-for-cup with all-purpose flour. Since whole-grain flours require more liquid, making a one-to-one switch without adding the appropriate amount of moisture can lead to a baked good with the texture of a brick. Follow the substitution guidelines below to get started. Because of their oil content, whole-grain flours can become rancid quickly. When they get old, they'll taste dank, musty, and mildewy. To preserve them for as long as possible, store them in the refrigerator or freezer. If you only use flour once a year, buy a new bag each year.

WHOLE-WHEAT PASTRY FLOUR: A finely milled soft wheat, whole-wheat pastry flour includes the entire grain in the flour, so it's more nutritious and contains more fiber than all-purpose flour. Whole-wheat pastry flour is much finer than regular whole-wheat flour. Substituting 50% of all-purpose flour with whole-wheat pastry flour is a great way to bump up nutrition and fiber while retaining the soft tenderness that is so wonderful in cakes.

EINKORN FLOUR: Cultivated over 12,000 years ago, einkorn wheat is grown today much the way it was then. The flour contains 80% of the whole grain. Keep the total amount of einkorn to 50% of the total flour in the recipe.

TEFF FLOUR: The tiny teff grain—about the size of a poppy seed—has a strong nutty, earthy flavor and is naturally gluten free. Substitute 25% of all-purpose flour with teff flour in baked goods to ensure the cake, bread, or cookie has the gluten structure to rise.

KAMUT FLOUR: In the last 20 years or so, growth in popularity and production of this grain has skyrocketed. Khorasan wheat, trademarked as Kamut, adds an earthy, sweet, and toasty flavor to baked goods. I love it because the flavor is wheaty without tasting overly grassy or earthy. Substitute up to 50% of all-purpose flour with Kamut.

AMARANTH FLOUR: High in protein and gluten free, amaranth adds a strong earthy, nutty, malty flavor to baked goods. Substitute about 25% of the all-purpose flour with amaranth flour.

NUT FLOURS: Nut flours and nut meals are really the same thing: nuts, with or without the skins left on, finely ground to an almost flour-like consistency. For a flavor boost, I usually toast nut flours before adding them to the other ingredients to draw out the essential oils. Store nut flours in an airtight container in the freezer. Substitute up to 25% of all-purpose flour with nut flour.

TOOLS I LOVE

I love kitchen gadgets so much that I have fallen prey to some pretty gimmicky stuff over the years. If you want a kitchen capable of handling any dessert, here are my must-have tools:

DIGITAL KITCHEN SCALE: A digital scale makes measuring flour and other ingredients listed by weight easy and quick to manage.

DRY AND LIQUID MEASURING CUPS: Yes, you need both for accuracy. Dry measuring cups measure the exact amount of dry ingredient. Liquid measuring cups have lines indicating amounts and usually feature a spout for pouring.

MEASURING SPOONS WITH NARROW BOWLS AND LONG HANDLES: These are easier to get inside small spice containers.

MIXING BOWLS IN VARIOUS SIZES: Purchase in stainless steel, glass, or plastic in a variety of sizes—2 cups up to 3 quarts work well.

WHISKS AND RUBBER SPATULAS: From itty-bitty to giant, spatulas are great for folding in light and airy ingredients. Whisks help blend together ingredients and add air to batters.

OFFSET METAL SPATULA: For icing cakes, cookies, and a million other uses, small and large metal offset spatulas tackle delicate jobs easily.

CHEF AND PARING KNIVES: Good sharp knives that fit your hand properly make tedious slicing, chopping, and peeling jobs easy.

SERRATED BREAD KNIFE: For cutting clean edges on cakes and loaves, a 12- to 14-inch serrated knife is great to have on hand.

INSTANT-READ THERMOMETER: This thermometer is essential for cooking sugar syrups and egg custards to their exact doneness.

CANDY THERMOMETER: Use a clip-on candy thermometer when making super-high temperature caramels and sugar syrups.

SERRATED PEELER: When peeling tender thin-skinned fruit, such as plums or apricots, a serrated peeler grabs the skin without gouging the fruit's juicy flesh.

MICROPLANE GRATER: Also called a zester, this grater is so sharp that it's easy to grate off only the thin yellow zest of a lemon.

ICE-CREAM SCOOPS: Keep a variety of sizes handy, such as 1 tablespoon (#60), 2 tablespoons (#30), ¼ cup (#16), and ⅓ cup (#12) for quick and consistent cookie and muffin portioning.

STRAIGHT-SIDED ROLLING PIN AND ROLLING PIN GUIDES: Rolling pin guides are handy and come in varying sizes to make rolling dough easy as, well, pie.

LIGHT-COLORED BAKING PANS: Stainless steel or aluminum baking pans conduct heat well for even browning. I avoid dark pans because they get hotter than the light-colored ones, making your baked goods turn out darker. These are the pans I reach for the most:

- 8-inch and 9-inch cake pans
- Standard 15 x 10–inch jelly-roll pan
- Rimmed and rimless baking sheets
- 9-inch springform pan
- 9-inch tart pan with removable bottom
- 9 x 5–inch loaf pan
- Mini (24-cup) and standard (12-cup) muffin pans
- 9-inch glass or ceramic pie dish (not deep-dish)
- 4-, 6-, and 8-ounce ramekins

STAND MIXER: The power of a stand mixer simply cannot be duplicated with a handheld mixer. It whips faster and stronger.

FOOD PROCESSOR: The lightening speed of the blade breaks down even the toughest nut.

THE
CAKE
WALK

CHOCOLATE CAKE
WITH VANILLA ITALIAN MERINGUE

Hands-on: 36 min. Total: 1 hr. 33 min.

½ cup boiling water
⅓ cup unsweetened cocoa
2 ounces bittersweet chocolate, finely chopped
11.25 ounces all-purpose flour (about 2½ cups)
1½ teaspoons baking powder
½ teaspoon baking soda
½ teaspoon salt
5 tablespoons unsalted butter, softened
3 tablespoons canola oil

1 cup sugar
½ teaspoon vanilla extract
2 large eggs
1 cup low-fat buttermilk
Baking spray with flour
½ cup sugar
3 tablespoons water
⅛ teaspoon salt
4 large egg whites, at room temperature
½ teaspoon cream of tartar
1 teaspoon vanilla extract

1. Preheat oven to 350°.

2. Combine first 3 ingredients in a small bowl; stir until smooth.

3. Weigh or lightly spoon flour into dry measuring cups; level with a knife. Combine flour and next 3 ingredients. Place butter and oil in a large bowl; beat with a mixer at medium speed 2 minutes or until combined. Add sugar and vanilla; beat until light and fluffy, about 3 minutes. Add eggs, 1 at a time, beating well after each addition. Add chocolate mixture; beat at low speed until just combined. Add flour mixture and buttermilk alternately to butter mixture, beginning and ending with flour mixture. Divide batter among 3 (8-inch) cake pans coated with baking spray. Bake at 350° for 17 minutes or until a wooden pick inserted in center comes out with moist crumbs clinging. Cool 10 minutes in pans on wire racks; remove from pans. Cool completely on wire racks.

4. Place ½ cup sugar, 3 tablespoons water, and ⅛ teaspoon salt in a small saucepan; bring to a boil, stirring until sugar melts. Cook 6 to 7 minutes or until a candy thermometer registers 230° (do not stir).

5. Place egg whites and cream of tartar in a large bowl; beat with a mixer at medium speed 2 minutes or until foamy. Increase mixer speed to high; beat 2 to 3 minutes or until soft peaks form. With mixer on low speed, pour hot syrup in a thin stream down the side of mixing bowl. Gradually increase the speed to high; beat 2 minutes or until stiff peaks form (do not overbeat). Add vanilla; beat until just combined.

6. Place 1 cake layer on a plate; spread top with about 1 cup icing. Repeat procedure with another cake layer. Top with remaining cake layer; spread remaining icing over top and sides of cake.

SERVES 14 (serving size: 1 slice)
CALORIES 278; FAT 9.6g (sat 4.4g, mono 3.4g, poly 1.2g); PROTEIN 5g; CARB 44g; FIBER 1g; CHOL 38mg; IRON 2mg; SODIUM 266mg; CALC 62mg

TECHNIQUE TIP

Combining the cocoa and chopped chocolate with boiling water accomplishes a couple of things: First, hydrating the powder in boiling water coaxes the essential flavors of the cocoa butter out of the powder, making the chocolate taste richer. Second, the boiling water melts the chopped chocolate so it blends easier into the cake batter.

MY TOP 5 TIPS FOR
MAKING CAKE

To me, baking a cake for a special occasion or for someone in particular is one of the greatest expressions of love imaginable. Your generous gift of time and energy— mixing, folding, icing, glazing, and getting the light and fluffy layers just right—will be remembered and appreciated.

1 *I know you have read and heard this tip over and over again, but it's so important that it's worth repeating: Read your recipe all the way through. By reading the recipe and understanding the different steps and the time each takes, you will be halfway there to a successful cake. Forgetting to preheat your oven is a sure way to ruin all your hard work to make that delicious cake batter.*

2 *Assemble and measure all your ingredients first. Getting in the habit of doing this will help you avoid discovering you are out of eggs at the exact moment you need to add them to the creamed butter and sugar mixture.*

3 *Prepare your cake pans and cooling racks. Baking spray with flour is simply the easiest way to assure an easy, clean release of cakes (and pies) from the simplest to the more intricately designed pan. Use it on cooling racks to help keep cakes from sticking after they have cooled. And for less mess and cleanup, spray the pans and the cooling racks over the open door of your dishwasher.*

4 *Don't take shortcuts. There are very good reasons for specific steps in cake recipes. If the recipe says to beat the butter and sugar together for 5 minutes, it's because the longer beating time will incorporate more air into the mixture, making the cake rise more. Or, alternating the addition of the dry ingredients with the liquid ingredients into the creamed butter mixture—why do this? A tender moist cake is the goal. (Who wants a dry or a crumbly cake?) Adding the flour alternately with the milk (or other liquid) to the creamed ingredients allows the flour to become coated with the fatty ingredients, which in turn makes the cake layers tender and meltingly soft.*

5 *I'm not a fan of artificial flavorings. And even natural extracts can be too much of a good thing. But if you do use extracts, such as coconut or almond, use them sparingly since their flavor can easily take over and make your cake have a chemical after-taste. I recommend starting with only ¼ teaspoon. Taste the batter, and then add more if you want a stronger flavor.*

1. Sweet overripe bananas with brown-speckled peels provide the best flavor for breads and cookies. So instead of tossing them in the trashcan, toss them (skin and all) in your freezer until you're ready to bake.

2. Thaw the bananas, without peeling them, in a dish at room temperature until they're soft. The longer the bananas are in the freezer, the darker the skin will become. Even though they may look rather ugly, their flesh will still be perfect to use.

3. Remove the peels and any overly brown spots on the bananas, and place them in a bowl. Mash the bananas with a fork, and measure out what you need.

BANANA LAYER CAKE
WITH BANANA LIQUEUR CURD

Hands-on: 35 min. Total: 1 hr. 15 min.

7.9 ounces all-purpose flour (about 1¾ cups)
1 teaspoon baking powder
½ teaspoon baking soda
½ teaspoon salt
¼ teaspoon freshly ground nutmeg
¾ cup sugar
¼ cup unsalted butter
2 tablespoons canola oil
2 large eggs
1 cup ripe mashed banana
¾ teaspoon vanilla extract

½ cup 2% reduced-fat milk
Baking spray with flour
½ cup sugar
1 tablespoon unsalted butter, softened
Dash of salt
3 large egg yolks
1 large egg
¾ cup 2% reduced-fat milk
2 tablespoons banana liqueur
¼ teaspoon vanilla extract
¼ cup chopped walnuts, toasted

1. Preheat oven to 350°.

2. Weigh or lightly spoon flour into dry measuring cups; level with a knife. Combine flour and next 4 ingredients in a bowl; stir with a whisk.

3. Place ¾ cup sugar, ¼ cup butter, and oil in a large bowl. Beat with a mixer at medium speed until well combined, about 3 minutes. Add eggs, 1 at a time, beating well after each addition. Add banana and vanilla; beat 1 minute or until combined. Add flour mixture and ½ cup milk alternately to butter mixture, beginning and ending with flour mixture. Divide batter evenly between 2 (8-inch) cake pans coated with baking spray. Bake at 350° for 20 minutes or until a wooden pick inserted in center comes out clean. Cool 10 minutes in pans on a wire rack; remove from pans. Cool completely on wire rack (about 30 minutes).

4. Place ½ cup sugar, 1 tablespoon butter, dash of salt, egg yolks, and egg in a small saucepan, stirring with a whisk until smooth. Stir in ¾ cup milk. Place pan over medium heat. Cook until a candy thermometer registers 160° and mixture has thickened, about 5 minutes, stirring constantly. Remove pan from heat. Stir in liqueur and vanilla. Pour mixture into a bowl. Place plastic wrap on surface of curd; chill (about 30 minutes).

5. Place 1 cake layer on a plate; spread with half of banana curd. Top with remaining cake layer; spread remaining curd over top of cake. Sprinkle evenly with nuts. Store cake covered in refrigerator.

SERVES 12 (serving size: 1 slice)

CALORIES 299; FAT 11.8g (sat 4.5g, mono 4.1g, poly 2.5g); PROTEIN 6g; CARB 42g; FIBER 1g; CHOL 107mg; IRON 1mg; SODIUM 235mg; CALC 73mg

PINEAPPLE UPSIDE-DOWN CAKE

Hands-on: 32 min. Total: 1 hr. 17 min.

I really like the flavor the ancient grain amaranth imparts to baked goods. It has malty, caramel, and sweet cereal notes that aren't found in everyday flours. It makes this cake hearty without it feeling heavy or overly dense.

7 tablespoons unsalted butter, divided
⅓ cup packed dark brown sugar
6 (½-inch-thick) slices fresh pineapple, patted dry
6 maraschino cherries, patted dry
9 ounces all-purpose flour (about 2 cups)
1.25 ounces amaranth flour (about ⅓ cup)
2 teaspoons baking powder
1 teaspoon baking soda
½ teaspoon salt
¾ cup granulated sugar
1 large egg
1 large egg yolk
1 teaspoon vanilla extract
1 cup 2% reduced-fat milk

1. Preheat oven to 425°.

2. Melt 3 tablespoons butter in a 10-inch cast-iron skillet. Add brown sugar; cook over medium heat 1 minute or until sugar almost melts, stirring constantly. Remove pan from heat. Arrange pineapple slices in pan; place 1 cherry in the center of each slice.

3. Weigh or lightly spoon flours into dry measuring cups; level with a knife. Combine flours and next 3 ingredients; stir with a whisk.

4. Place ¼ cup butter and granulated sugar in a bowl; beat with a mixer at medium speed until light and fluffy, about 2 minutes. Add egg and egg yolk, 1 at a time, beating well after each addition. Add vanilla; beat until combined. Add flour mixture and milk alternately to butter mixture, beginning and ending with flour mixture. Scrape batter into prepared pan; smooth top with a spatula. Bake at 425° for 5 minutes. (Don't worry, the batter shouldn't spill over; but if you like, you can always place a baking sheet on the rack below.) Reduce oven temperature to 350°. Bake at 350° for 25 minutes or until a wooden pick inserted in center comes out clean. Cool 10 minutes in pan on a wire rack. Place a plate upside down on top of pan; invert cake onto plate. Serve warm or at room temperature.

SERVES 12 (serving size: 1 wedge)
CALORIES 255; FAT 8.3g (sat 4.9g, mono 2.2g, poly 0.5g); PROTEIN 4g; CARB 42g; FIBER 1g; CHOL 50mg; IRON 1mg; SODIUM 302mg; CALC 88mg

MARASCHINO CHERRIES

These sweetened cherries are typically made from sweet cherry varieties, such as Royal Ann, Rainier, or Gold. Many brands brine the cherries in a solution that bleaches them, and then soak them in a mixture of food coloring (usually Red Dye #40) and sugar syrup (containing high-fructose corn syrup) to give them their ruby-red hue. However, there are all-natural brands available that don't have artificial colors, dyes, or flavors added, such as Tillen Farms, that you can use.

RUM-RAISIN BUNDT CAKE

Hands-on: 35 min. Total: 1 hr. 35 min.

Dark spicy rum adds a nice kick to this cake, but if you'd prefer not to use it you can easily substitute the same amount of apple juice or orange juice. Instead of one large Bundt cake, you can make 12 mini cakes: Just spoon the batter evenly among 12 mini Bundt molds that have been well coated with baking spray. Bake them at 350° for about 18 minutes or until a wooden pick comes out clean.

½ cup golden raisins
3 tablespoons dark rum
   (such as Myers's Dark Rum)
10 ounces cake flour
   (about 2½ cups)
2 teaspoons baking powder
½ teaspoon baking soda
½ teaspoon salt
¼ cup unsalted butter, softened
¼ cup canola oil
1 cup granulated sugar, divided

1 tablespoon grated orange rind
1 tablespoon grated lemon rind
2 teaspoons vanilla extract
2 large eggs
¾ cup 2% reduced-fat milk
Baking spray with flour
2 tablespoons water
1 tablespoon light-colored corn
   syrup
1 tablespoon powdered sugar

1. Preheat oven to 350°.

2. Combine raisins and rum in a small microwave-safe bowl; microwave at HIGH 30 seconds. Cool to room temperature. (This softens the raisins. Plus, they absorb some of the rum for a boost of flavor.)

3. Weigh or lightly spoon flour into dry measuring cups; level with a knife. Combine flour and next 3 ingredients (through salt) in a bowl; stir with a whisk. Place butter, oil, and ¾ cup sugar in a large bowl; beat with a mixer at medium speed until smooth. Beat in rinds and vanilla. Add eggs, 1 at a time, beating well after each addition. Add flour mixture and milk alternately to butter mixture, beginning and ending with flour mixture. Drain raisins through a sieve over a bowl; reserve rum. Stir raisins into batter. Pour batter into a 10-cup Bundt pan coated with baking spray. Bake at 350° for 40 minutes or until a wooden pick inserted in center comes out clean. Cool 10 minutes in pan on a wire rack. Place a plate upside down on top of cake; invert onto plate.

4. Combine ¼ cup sugar, 2 tablespoons water, and corn syrup in a small saucepan; bring to a boil. Cook 1 minute. Remove pan from heat; stir in reserved rum. Brush syrup over warm cake. Cool completely. Sprinkle top with powdered sugar.

SERVES 12 (serving size: 1 wedge)

CALORIES 282; FAT 9.8g (sat 3.3g, mono 4.4g, poly 1.7g); PROTEIN 4g; CARB 43g; FIBER 1g; CHOL 42mg; IRON 2mg; SODIUM 253mg; CALC 78mg

ALMOND AND ORANGE SEMOLINA CAKES

Hands-on: 35 min. Total: 2 hr.

3.75 ounces almond flour
(about 1 cup)
8 ounces all-purpose flour
(about 1¾ cups)
5.5 ounces semolina flour
(about 1 cup)
2 teaspoons baking powder
½ teaspoon baking soda
¼ teaspoon salt
½ cup unsalted butter
1½ cups sugar, divided
2 tablespoons grated orange
rind, divided
1¾ teaspoons vanilla extract,
divided
4 large eggs
1 cup plain (full-fat) yogurt
Baking spray with flour
¾ cup fresh orange juice
¼ cup orange liqueur (such as
Grand Marnier; optional)

1. Preheat oven to 350°.

2. Weigh or lightly spoon almond flour into a dry measuring cup; level with a knife. Spread on a baking sheet. Bake at 350° for 6 minutes or until it is beginning to brown and become fragrant, stirring after 3 minutes. Cool to room temperature on pan.

3. Weigh or lightly spoon all-purpose and semolina flours into dry measuring cups; level with a knife. Combine flours and next 3 ingredients (through salt) in a bowl, stirring with a whisk.

4. Place butter and 1¼ cups sugar in a large bowl; beat at medium speed 3 minutes or until well combined. Add 1 tablespoon rind and 1½ teaspoons vanilla; beat until combined. Add eggs, 1 at a time, beating well after each addition. Add flour mixture; beat at low speed 1 minute or until just combined. Add yogurt; beat 1 minute or until just combined. Scrape batter into 4 (6 x 3–inch) mini loaf pans coated with baking spray. Bake at 350° for 25 to 30 minutes or until a wooden pick inserted in center comes out completely dry.

5. Combine ¼ cup sugar, 1 tablespoon rind, and orange juice in a small saucepan; bring to a boil. Remove pan from heat; stir in ¼ teaspoon vanilla and liqueur, if desired. Pierce surfaces of cakes liberally with a skewer; drizzle half of glaze over cakes. Let stand 15 minutes. Loosen cakes from sides of pans using a narrow metal spatula. Invert onto plates. Pierce tops of cakes liberally with a skewer; drizzle remaining glaze over cakes. Serve cakes at room temperature.

SERVES 16 (serving size: 1 slice)
CALORIES 298; FAT 11g (sat 4.5g, mono 4.2g, poly 1.4g); PROTEIN 7g;
CARB 42g; FIBER 2g; CHOL 63mg; IRON 2mg; SODIUM 169mg; CALC 92mg

TECHNIQUE TIP

Adding a combination of orange liqueur, orange rind, and juice provides big, bright flavor. Using zest is an easy way to boost citrus flavor without adding more liquid to the cake. This cake also bakes easily in a 10-cup Bundt pan. Increase the bake time to 40 minutes, checking doneness with a wooden pick after 35 minutes.

FRESH GINGER CAKE
WITH CANDIED CITRUS GLAZE

Hands-on: 30 min. Total: 1 hr. 20 min.

If you've ever wandered down the international food aisle in your grocery store, you might have seen Lyle's Golden Syrup in the green and gold can. Lyle's syrup is thick and lightly caramelized and can be used on pancakes and French toast or in recipes where light-colored corn syrup is used. The flavor is incredible—it has buttery, caramel notes—and it adds extra moisture to baked goods. If kumquats are not in season, substitute orange or lemon rind (whichever you prefer). Use a vegetable peeler to cut the rind into 1-inch strips (no pith!), cut the strips into ¼-inch slices to equal about ½ cup, and then prepare them the same way as the kumquats in step 4.

CAKE:
11.25 ounces all-purpose flour
  (about 2½ cups)
1 teaspoon baking powder
½ teaspoon baking soda
¼ teaspoon salt
⅔ cup golden cane syrup
  (such as Lyle's Golden Syrup)
½ cup canola oil
½ cup reduced-fat sour cream
⅓ cup sugar
3 tablespoons unsalted butter,
  melted and cooled

3 tablespoons grated peeled
  fresh ginger
3 large eggs
⅔ cup ginger ale, at room
  temperature
Baking spray with flour

GLAZE:
1 cup kumquats, thinly sliced
  and seeded
1 cup water
⅔ cup sugar
Dash of salt

1. Preheat oven to 350°.

2. To prepare cake, weigh or lightly spoon flour into dry measuring cups; level with a knife. Combine flour and next 3 ingredients (through salt) in a bowl, stirring with a whisk.

3. Combine syrup and next 6 ingredients (through eggs) in a large bowl; beat with a mixer at low speed 1 minute or until well combined. Add flour mixture and ginger ale alternately to syrup mixture, beginning and ending with flour mixture. Pour batter into a 10-cup Bundt pan coated with baking spray. Bake at 350° for 35 minutes or until a wooden pick inserted in center comes out clean. Cool 15 minutes in pan on a wire rack. Place a plate upside down on top of cake; invert cake onto plate.

4. To prepare glaze, place kumquats, 1 cup water, ⅔ cup sugar, and dash of salt in a saucepan; bring to a boil. Simmer, uncovered, until reduced to ⅔ cup, about 18 minutes, stirring occasionally. Drizzle glaze over warm cake.

SERVES 14 (serving size: 1 wedge)
CALORIES 298; FAT 12.8g (sat 3.2g, mono 6.4g, poly 2.7g); PROTEIN 4g; CARB 48g; FIBER 1g; CHOL 50mg; IRON 1mg; SODIUM 204mg; CALC 42mg

HUMMINGBIRD MINI BUNDT CAKES
WITH BOURBON GLAZE

Hands-on: 20 min. Total: 43 min.

The hummingbird cake has been around Southern homes for decades. Adding bourbon to the glaze is my nod to Southern proclivities, but you can substitute the same amount of pineapple or orange juice for the bourbon, if you like.

TECHNIQUE TIP

These minis can easily be made into one large Bundt. Just pour the batter into a 10-cup Bundt pan coated with baking spray, and bake at 350° for about 40 minutes or until a wooden pick comes out clean.

10.1 ounces all-purpose flour (about 2¼ cups)
2 teaspoons baking powder
1½ teaspoons ground cinnamon
½ teaspoon baking soda
½ teaspoon salt
¾ cup granulated sugar
¼ cup unsalted butter
2 tablespoons canola oil
2 large eggs
1¼ teaspoons vanilla extract, divided
½ cup low-fat buttermilk
1 cup chopped banana (about 1 large)
½ cup chopped pecans, toasted
1 (8-ounce) can crushed pineapple (packed in its own juice), undrained
Baking spray with flour
½ cup powdered sugar
1 tablespoon bourbon
1 tablespoon unsalted butter, melted

1. Preheat oven to 350°.

2. Weigh or lightly spoon flour into dry measuring cups; level with a knife. Combine flour and next 4 ingredients (through salt) in a bowl; stir with a whisk. Place granulated sugar, butter, and canola oil in a large bowl; beat with a mixer at medium speed until well combined, about 4 minutes. Add eggs, 1 at a time, beating well after each addition. Beat in 1 teaspoon vanilla. Add flour mixture and buttermilk alternately to sugar mixture, beginning and ending with flour mixture. Fold in banana, nuts, and pineapple.

3. Divide batter evenly among 12 mini Bundt pans coated with baking spray. Bake at 350° for 18 to 19 minutes or until a wooden pick inserted in center comes out clean. Cool 5 minutes in pans on a wire rack; remove from pans.

4. Combine ¼ teaspoon vanilla, powdered sugar, bourbon, and melted butter in a small bowl; stir with a whisk until smooth. Drizzle glaze over warm cakes.

SERVES 12 (serving size: 1 cake)
CALORIES 292; FAT 11.6g (sat 3.9g, mono 4.9g, poly 2.1g); PROTEIN 5g; CARB 43g; FIBER 2g; CHOL 44mg; IRON 2mg; SODIUM 264mg; CALC 76mg

LEMON SOUR CREAM POUND CAKE

WITH FRESH STRAWBERRY SAUCE

Hands-on: 14 min. Total: 1 hr. 27 min.

If you're making this dessert ahead, wait until just before you're serving it to spoon on the strawberry sauce so the cake doesn't become soggy. Try the sauce right off the stove—hot strawberries are a delightful change.

10.1 ounces all-purpose flour
   (about 2¼ cups)
1¾ teaspoons baking powder
½ teaspoon baking soda
½ teaspoon salt
1 cup sugar
¼ cup unsalted butter, softened
2 tablespoons canola oil
1 large egg
1 large egg yolk
2 teaspoons grated lemon rind

2 tablespoons fresh lemon juice
1 teaspoon vanilla extract
1 cup reduced-fat sour cream
¼ cup 2% reduced-fat milk
Baking spray with flour
2 cups chopped fresh
   strawberries (about 1 pound)
¼ cup sugar
1 tablespoon cornstarch
1 tablespoon fresh lemon juice
Dash of salt

1. Preheat oven to 350°.

2. Weigh or lightly spoon flour into dry measuring cups; level with a knife. Combine flour and next 3 ingredients (through salt) in a bowl, stirring with a whisk. Place 1 cup sugar, butter, and oil in a bowl; beat with a mixer at medium speed 3 minutes or until light and fluffy. Add egg and egg yolk, 1 at a time, beating well after each addition. Beat in lemon rind, lemon juice, and vanilla. Combine sour cream and milk in a bowl, stirring with a whisk until smooth. Add flour mixture and sour cream mixture alternately to butter mixture, beginning and ending with flour mixture, beating until just combined. Spoon batter into a 9 x 5–inch loaf pan coated with baking spray. Bake at 350° for 55 minutes or until a wooden pick inserted in center comes out clean. Cool 10 minutes in pan on a wire rack. Remove from pan; cool on wire rack.

3. Combine strawberries and remaining ingredients in a saucepan; bring to a boil. Reduce heat, and cook 2 minutes or until thick and bubbly, mashing strawberries with a potato masher or a fork. Spoon sauce over cake.

SERVES 12 (serving size: 1 slice and about 2 tablespoons sauce)
CALORIES 281; FAT 9.6g (sat 4.3g, mono 3.5g, poly 1.2g); PROTEIN 4g;
CARB 45g; FIBER 1g; CHOL 49mg; IRON 1mg; SODIUM 260mg; CALC 91mg

SOUR CREAM

When sour cream is added to the cake, it makes the texture richer, denser, and more flavorful. From the chemistry side, the tangy acid in the sour cream reacts with the baking soda to create the gas to help the cake rise to its full potential.

VANILLA ANGEL FOOD CAKE
WITH DARK CHOCOLATE SAUCE

Hands-on: 40 min. Total: 1 hr. 30 min.

4 ounces cake flour (about 1 cup)
1¾ cups sugar, divided
12 large egg whites, at room temperature
1 teaspoon cream of tartar
¼ teaspoon salt
1¾ teaspoons vanilla extract, divided

¾ cup whole milk
¼ cup half-and-half
Dash of salt
2 ounces bittersweet chocolate, finely chopped
1 teaspoon cornstarch
1 large egg yolk

1. Preheat oven to 350°.

2. Weigh or lightly spoon flour into a dry measuring cup; level with a knife. Sift together flour and ¾ cup sugar.

3. Place egg whites, cream of tartar, and salt in a large bowl; beat with a mixer at medium speed until foamy (about 1 minute). Increase speed to high; beat until soft peaks form, about 2 minutes. With mixer at medium speed, add ¾ cup sugar, 1 tablespoon at a time. Beat until medium peaks form, about 2 minutes (do not overbeat). Add 1½ teaspoons vanilla, and beat until just combined.

4. Sift ¼ cup flour mixture over top of egg white mixture; gently fold in. Repeat procedure with remaining flour mixture, ¼ cup at a time, being careful not to deflate egg whites. Spoon batter into an ungreased 10-inch tube pan, spreading evenly. Bake at 350° for 40 minutes or until cake springs back when lightly touched. Invert pan over the neck of a glass bottle (so the cake is hanging upside down); cool cake completely. Loosen cake from sides of pan using a narrow metal spatula. Invert cake onto a plate; invert again.

5. Combine milk, half-and-half, 2 tablespoons sugar, dash of salt, and chocolate in a small saucepan; bring to a simmer, stirring until mixture is smooth. Place 2 tablespoons sugar, cornstarch, and egg yolk in a bowl, and stir well with a whisk. Gradually add hot milk mixture to egg mixture, stirring constantly with a whisk. Return milk mixture to pan. Cook over medium heat until mixture boils, stirring constantly. Remove from heat. Stir in ¼ teaspoon vanilla. Serve cake with warm sauce.

SERVES 12 (serving size: 1 slice and about 1½ tablespoons sauce)
CALORIES 212; FAT 2.7g (sat 2g, mono 0.5g, poly 0.2g); PROTEIN 5g; CARB 41g; FIBER 0g; CHOL 19mg; IRON 1mg; SODIUM 131mg; CALC 28mg

1. Beating the egg whites, cream of tartar, and salt until foamy at a lower speed first builds strong bubbles that will help the cake expand in the oven without collapsing.

2. Add the remaining sugar slowly and a little at a time when the whites reach soft peaks so that it doesn't break the air bubbles.

3. If your angel food cake pan doesn't have feet to suspend it upside down, use the neck of a sturdy bottle, like a wine bottle, to hang the pan upside down until the cake is completely cool. Hanging the cake upside down helps prevent the cake from collapsing or sinking.

EGGNOG COFFEE CAKE

Hands-on: 15 min. Total: 60 min.

This coffee cake is rich with egg yolks and the heady fragrance of freshly grated nutmeg. I do recommend grating your own nutmeg, since fresh spices are key to flavorful and memorable treats. A Microplane grater-zester works wonderfully well on the hard-as-nails whole nutmeg.

¼ cup old-fashioned rolled oats
¼ cup packed brown sugar
3 tablespoons all-purpose flour
⅛ teaspoon salt
2 tablespoons unsalted butter, chilled
¼ cup chopped pecans, toasted
6.75 ounces all-purpose flour (about 1½ cups)
1½ teaspoons freshly ground nutmeg
1 teaspoon baking powder
½ teaspoon baking soda
¼ teaspoon salt
½ cup granulated sugar
3 tablespoons unsalted butter, softened
1 large egg
1 large egg yolk
½ cup 2% reduced-fat milk
¼ cup reduced-fat sour cream
1½ teaspoons vanilla extract
Baking spray with flour

1. Preheat oven to 350°.

2. Combine first 4 ingredients in a bowl, stirring with a whisk. Cut in 2 tablespoons chilled butter using a pastry cutter or 2 knives until mixture resembles coarse meal (or follow the advice in the technique tip). Stir in nuts.

3. Weigh or lightly spoon flour into dry measuring cups; level with a knife. Combine flour and next 4 ingredients; stir with a whisk. Place granulated sugar and 3 tablespoons softened butter in a medium bowl; beat with a mixer at medium speed 4 minutes or until well combined. Add egg and egg yolk, 1 at a time, beating well after each addition. Add milk, sour cream, and vanilla; beat at low speed 1 minute or until well combined. Add flour mixture; beat at low speed until just combined.

4. Spoon half of batter into an 8-inch round cake pan coated with baking spray. Sprinkle with half of crumble mixture. Spread remaining half of batter over crumble, smoothing top with a spatula. Sprinkle top with remaining half of crumble. Bake at 350° for 25 to 30 minutes or until a wooden pick inserted in center comes out clean. Cool 15 minutes in pan on a wire rack. Place a plate upside down on top of cake; invert cake onto plate. Place another plate upside down on top of cake; invert onto plate.

SERVES 10 (serving size: 1 wedge)

CALORIES 266; FAT 10g (sat 4.8g, mono 3.3g, poly 1.2g); PROTEIN 4g; CARB 40g; FIBER 1g; CHOL 55mg; IRON 1mg; SODIUM 221mg; CALC 68mg

TECHNIQUE TIP

Here's a trick for making streusel or crumble toppings: Place the amount of butter the recipe calls for in the freezer while you're preheating the oven and preparing the cake batter. By the time you need it, it will be nice and solid and easy to grate on a box grater. Then all you need to do is toss it with the remaining streusel ingredients for an easy mix.

KAMUT-APPLE SNACK CAKE

Hands-on: 24 min. Total: 1 hr. 19 min.

There are many ways to describe Kamut flour's unique flavor attributes: earthy, sweet, toasty. It adds all those elements to this cake. If you absolutely can't find it, substitute whole-wheat pastry flour. Baking this cake at a lower temperature gives the apples time to get tender, and the moisture in the apples keeps the cake from drying out.

CAKE:
1 cup granulated sugar
1/4 cup unsalted butter, melted and cooled
2 tablespoons canola oil
1 teaspoon vanilla extract
2 large eggs
3.4 ounces Kamut flour (about 3/4 cup)
3.4 ounces all-purpose flour (about 3/4 cup)
1 teaspoon baking powder
1 teaspoon ground cinnamon
1/2 teaspoon baking soda
1/4 teaspoon salt
1/4 teaspoon freshly ground nutmeg
2 cups (1/2-inch) diced apple (about 1 large Golden Delicious or Honey Crisp)
Baking spray with flour

STREUSEL:
1/4 cup packed brown sugar
2 tablespoons all-purpose flour
2 tablespoons quick-cooking oats
2 tablespoons chopped walnuts
2 tablespoons frozen unsalted butter, grated
1/4 teaspoon ground cinnamon
Dash of salt

1. Preheat oven to 325°.

2. To prepare cake, place first 5 ingredients in a large bowl; beat with a mixer at medium speed 30 seconds or until well combined. Weigh or lightly spoon flours into dry measuring cups; level with a knife. Combine flours and next 5 ingredients (through nutmeg) in a bowl; stir with a whisk. Add flour mixture to sugar mixture; beat at low speed until just combined (batter is very thick). Stir in apple by hand. Spread batter into a 9-inch springform pan coated with baking spray.

3. To prepare streusel, combine brown sugar and remaining ingredients in a small bowl; toss to combine. Sprinkle streusel topping evenly over top of batter. Bake at 325° for 45 minutes or until a wooden pick inserted in center comes out clean. Cool 10 minutes in pan; remove sides from pan. Cool completely or serve warm.

SERVES 10 (serving size: 1 wedge)
CALORIES 299; FAT 12g (sat 5g, mono 4.1g, poly 2g); PROTEIN 4g; CARB 46g; FIBER 2g; CHOL 56mg; IRON 1mg; SODIUM 216mg; CALC 48mg

PEANUT BUTTER AND CHOCOLATE SWIRL LOAF CAKE

Hands-on: 24 min. Total: 1 hr. 49 min.

Peanut butter and chocolate, an all-time favorite flavor combination, are gently swirled together in this moist loaf cake. Using the edge of a knife to create the swirl helps keep the two batters from mixing together too much. Use your preferred peanut butter—crunchy or creamy, natural or commercially produced. All work beautifully.

CHOCOLATE SWIRL:
⅓ cup granulated sugar
¼ cup unsweetened cocoa
¼ cup water

CAKE:
6 ounces all-purpose flour
   (about 1⅓ cups)
1 teaspoon baking powder
½ teaspoon baking soda
¾ cup packed brown sugar
½ cup creamy peanut butter

¼ cup unsalted butter, softened
½ teaspoon salt
1 large egg
1 large egg yolk
1 teaspoon vanilla extract
¾ cup 2% reduced-fat milk
Baking spray with flour

DRIZZLE:
¼ cup powdered sugar
2 teaspoons water

1. Preheat oven to 350°.

2. To prepare swirl, combine first 3 ingredients in a medium bowl, stirring until smooth.

3. To prepare cake, weigh or lightly spoon flour into dry measuring cups; level with a knife. Combine flour and next 3 ingredients (through salt) in a bowl; stir with a whisk. Place brown sugar, peanut butter, and butter in a large bowl. Beat with a mixer at medium speed until well combined, about 3 minutes. Add egg and egg yolk, 1 at a time, beating well after each addition. Beat in vanilla. Add flour mixture and milk alternately to butter mixture, beginning and ending with flour mixture. Remove 1 cup peanut butter batter; add to chocolate swirl mixture, stirring until combined. Layer half of peanut butter batter in bottom of a 9 x 5–inch loaf pan coated with baking spray; top with half of chocolate batter, carefully smoothing to edge of pan. Repeat layers with remaining batters. Swirl batters together using a knife. Bake at 350° for 50 minutes or until a wooden pick inserted in center comes out clean. Cool 10 minutes in pan on a wire rack. Remove from pan; cool completely on wire rack.

4. To prepare drizzle, stir together powdered sugar and 2 teaspoons water until smooth; drizzle over top of cooled cake.

SERVES 12 (serving size: 1 slice)
CALORIES 256; FAT 10.7g (sat 4.2g, mono 4.1g, poly 1.9g); PROTEIN 6g;
CARB 37g; FIBER 2g; CHOL 42mg; IRON 1mg; SODIUM 258mg; CALC 67mg

CHOCOLATE CAKES
WITH CHOCOLATE SAUCE AND SWISS MERINGUE

Hands-on: 35 min. Total: 1 hr. 35 min.

Cooking spray
1 cup sugar, divided
¾ cup water, divided
2 tablespoons unsalted butter, melted and cooled
3 large eggs, separated
2 ounces cake flour (about ½ cup)
Dash of salt
⅓ cup plus 2 tablespoons unsweetened cocoa, divided
1 tablespoon unsalted butter
½ teaspoon cake flour
2 large egg whites, at room temperature
¼ teaspoon cream of tartar
Mint leaves (optional)

1. Preheat oven to 350°. Coat 6 (8-ounce) ramekins with cooking spray. Sprinkle ramekins evenly with 3 tablespoons sugar, tapping out excess.

2. Combine ¼ cup plus 1 tablespoon sugar, ½ cup water, 2 tablespoons melted butter, and 3 egg yolks in a large bowl, stirring with a whisk. Weigh or lightly spoon flour into a dry measuring cup; level with a knife. Combine flour, salt, and ⅓ cup cocoa in a bowl, stirring with a whisk. Add flour mixture to yolk mixture, stirring until well combined (mixture will look a little grainy).

3. Beat 3 egg whites with a mixer at medium speed until foamy. Gradually add ¼ cup sugar, 1 tablespoon at a time. Beat mixture at high speed until soft peaks form. Gently stir one-fourth of egg white mixture into batter; gently fold in remaining egg white mixture. Divide batter evenly among prepared ramekins; place ramekins on a baking sheet. Bake at 350° for 22 to 24 minutes or until a wooden pick inserted in center comes out clean. Cool completely on a wire rack. Run a knife around edge of ramekins; carefully remove cakes.

4. Combine ¼ cup water, 2 tablespoons sugar, 2 tablespoons cocoa, 1 tablespoon butter, and ½ teaspoon flour in a small saucepan. Cook 2 minutes or until thick and bubbly, stirring constantly with a whisk.

5. Combine 2 egg whites, 2 tablespoons sugar, and cream of tartar in the top of a double boiler, stirring with a whisk. Cook over simmering water until sugar dissolves, stirring constantly with a whisk, until a candy thermometer registers 160°, about 2 minutes. Pour mixture into a medium bowl. Beat with a mixer with clean, dry beaters at high speed until stiff peaks form, about 2 minutes. To serve, top each cake with about 1½ tablespoons chocolate sauce and a dollop of meringue. Top with a mint leaf, if desired. Serve immediately.

SERVES 6 (serving size: 1 cake)
CALORIES 272; FAT 9.1g (sat 5g, mono 2.7g, poly 0.8g); PROTEIN 6g; CARB 45g; FIBER 2g; CHOL 108mg; IRON 2mg; SODIUM 81mg; CALC 27mg

1. Place the egg whites, sugar, and cream of tartar together in the top of a double boiler, whisking until well combined. (If you don't have a double boiler, you can create one by setting a metal mixing bowl over a saucepan of simmering water. Just be sure the bottom of the bowl doesn't touch the water.)

2. Place the mixture over simmering water, and cook until a candy thermometer registers about 160°, whisking constantly, until the sugar crystals melt completely.

3. Be sure to use clean, dry beaters when beating the egg whites to ensure they whip to maximum volume. Even a speck of fat can have an effect.

MY TOP 5 TIPS FOR MAKING MERINGUE

Meringue is made of egg whites, cream of tartar, and granulated sugar. How they're combined dictates how they're used.

1 *The egg whites need to be at room temperature and cannot contain ANY of the sunny yellow egg yolk. The fat in the yolks will sabotage the meringue, preventing the whites from whipping into billowy clouds.*

2 *Make sure your bowl and beaters are perfectly clean and free of leftover oils or fats. That, too, can prevent the meringue from reaching its full capacity.*

3 *Begin mixing the egg whites on medium-low speed. The lower speed begins to build bubbles, and they'll gradually increase in number and volume. Then increase the speed to high, which will create even smaller bubbles that will be stronger and better able to withstand additional expansion in the oven or when folded into batter.*

4 *Adding cream of tartar (an acid) adds additional strength to the bubbles, helping them expand and not collapse.*

5 *If adding vanilla extract, add it after the meringue is fully whipped. Adding it too soon could limit the meringue's volume.*

French meringue is made of uncooked egg whites, cream of tartar, and granulated sugar. Use it to top pies where the filling is hot and the pie goes in the oven to lightly brown the meringue on top; this ensures that the whites are cooked all the way through from the bottom to the top. French meringue is also folded into cake batters to act as a leavener.

Italian meringue is egg whites and cream of tartar whipped until medium peaks form. Boiling hot sugar syrup (about 234° to 240°) is drizzled down the side of the bowl, and then the mixture is whipped until firm peaks form and it cools to room temperature. The hot syrup cooks the egg whites and makes the meringue stable and ready to ice a cake, top a pie, or fold into mousse.

Swiss meringue is made by continuously whisking together egg whites, cream of tartar, and sugar over simmering water until the sugar crystals melt and the mixture reaches 160°. The mixture is then taken off the heat and whipped until firm peaks form. Swiss meringue can be folded into mousse, cake batters, and buttercreams without fear of collapsing.

Stable Italian and Swiss meringues can be shaped and baked into cookies, spirals for layered desserts, and sculpted nests for Pavlovas.

MAPLE CUPCAKES
WITH MAPLE–BROWN SUGAR ICING

Hands-on: 17 min. Total: 52 min.

For the biggest maple punch, use medium or dark amber grade syrup that has richer, deeper maple flavor. Don't let your cupcakes linger too long in the pan while they are cooling. The heat gets trapped and can lead to a soggy-bottomed cupcake.

CUPCAKES:
6.75 ounces all-purpose flour
   (about 1½ cups)
1 teaspoon baking powder
¼ teaspoon baking soda
¼ teaspoon salt
⅓ cup maple syrup (grade B)
¼ cup packed brown sugar
¼ cup unsalted butter
2 tablespoons canola oil
2 large eggs
1 teaspoon vanilla extract
½ cup low-fat buttermilk

ICING:
3 tablespoons maple syrup
   (grade B)
2 tablespoons unsalted butter
2 tablespoons brown sugar
1½ cups powdered sugar
¼ teaspoon vanilla extract
⅛ teaspoon salt

1. Preheat oven to 350°.

2. To prepare cupcakes, weigh or lightly spoon flour into dry measuring cups; level with a knife. Combine flour and next 3 ingredients (through salt) in a bowl; stir with a whisk.

3. Place syrup, brown sugar, butter, and oil in a large bowl. Beat with a mixer at medium speed until light and fluffy, about 3 minutes. Add eggs, 1 at a time, beating well after each addition. Beat in vanilla. Add flour mixture and buttermilk alternately to butter mixture, beginning and ending with flour mixture. Divide batter evenly among 12 muffin cups lined with cupcake liners. Bake at 350° for 17 minutes or until a wooden pick inserted in center comes out clean. Cool 5 minutes in pans on a wire rack; remove from pans. Cool completely on wire racks.

4. To prepare icing, place syrup, butter, and brown sugar in a medium microwave-safe bowl. Microwave at HIGH 30 seconds or until butter melts. Stir until smooth. Add powdered sugar, vanilla, and salt; stir with a whisk until smooth. Spread about 1 tablespoon icing on top of each cupcake.

SERVES 12 (serving size: 1 cupcake)
CALORIES 267; FAT 9.1g (sat 4.2g, mono 3.3g, poly 1.1g); PROTEIN 3g;
CARB 44g; FIBER 0g; CHOL 47mg; IRON 1mg; SODIUM 167mg; CALC 63mg

SERIOUSLY CHOCOLATE CUPCAKES

Hands-on: 31 min. Total: 1 hr. 19 min.

½ cup boiling water
½ cup dark unsweetened cocoa, divided
2 ounces bittersweet chocolate, finely chopped
¼ teaspoon instant coffee (optional)
5.6 ounces all-purpose flour (about 1¼ cups)
1 teaspoon baking powder
⅜ teaspoon salt, divided
¼ teaspoon baking soda

1 cup granulated sugar
¼ cup plus 1 tablespoon unsalted butter, softened and divided
2 tablespoons canola oil
2 large eggs
1¼ teaspoons vanilla extract, divided
¼ cup 2% reduced-fat milk
2 ounces ⅓-less-fat cream cheese, softened
1 tablespoon 2% reduced-fat milk
1½ cups powdered sugar

1. Preheat oven to 350°.

2. Combine ½ cup boiling water, ¼ cup cocoa, bittersweet chocolate, and coffee, if desired, in a small bowl, stirring until smooth. Set aside.

3. Weigh or lightly spoon flour into dry measuring cups; level with a knife. Combine flour, baking powder, ¼ teaspoon salt, and baking soda in a bowl; stir with a whisk.

4. Place granulated sugar, ¼ cup butter, and oil in a large bowl. Beat with a mixer at medium speed until light and fluffy, about 3 minutes. Add eggs, 1 at a time, beating well after each addition. Add 1 teaspoon vanilla and chocolate mixture; beat at low speed just until combined. Add flour mixture and ¼ cup milk alternately to butter mixture, beginning and ending with flour mixture. Divide batter among 12 muffin cups lined with cupcake liners. (Liners will be almost full.) Bake at 350° for 18 minutes or until a wooden pick inserted in center comes out clean. Cool 5 minutes in pans on a wire rack; remove from pans. Cool completely on wire rack.

5. Place cream cheese, 1 tablespoon butter, milk, ¼ teaspooon vanilla, and ⅛ teaspooon salt in a medium bowl. Beat with a mixer at low speed until smooth, about 3 minutes. Whisk together powdered sugar and ¼ cup cocoa; add to cream cheese mixture. Beat at low speed until smooth. Spread about 1½ tablespoons icing on each cupcake.

SERVES 12 (serving size: 1 cupcake)
CALORIES 290; FAT 11g (sat 5.3g, mono 3.4g, poly 1.1g); PROTEIN 4g;
CARB 47g; FIBER 1g; CHOL 48mg; IRON 1mg; SODIUM 218mg; CALC 46mg

TECHNIQUE TIP

Dark cocoa isn't for every recipe. Using just a little in these cupcakes deepens the color, but care must be taken. I discovered that using too much in a baked good will turn it army gray or even purple! And, by adding just a little instant coffee, the chocolate flavor intensifies.

MILE-HIGH COCONUT CUPCAKES

Hands-on: 22 min. Total: 1 hr. 10 min.

Coconut is delicious, but it's also high in saturated fat. Instead of using coconut extract to help these cupcakes stay on the lighter side, I prefer to use the real stuff in moderation. (Some extracts and artificial flavorings taste like chemicals or really bad medicine.) To get maximum flavor out of a small amount, I infused the coconut milk with flaked coconut and toasted the coconut that gets sprinkled on top of the icing. Infusing and toasting ekes out every possible bit of coconut flavor.

CUPCAKES:
3/4 cup canned light coconut milk
7 tablespoons flaked sweetened
  coconut, divided
1 vanilla bean, halved lengthwise
6.75 ounces all-purpose flour
  (about 1 1/2 cups)
1 teaspoon baking powder
1/2 teaspoon baking soda
1/4 teaspoon salt
3/4 cup sugar
6 tablespoons unsalted butter,
  softened

2 tablespoons canola oil
3 large egg whites
1/2 teaspoon cream of tartar

ICING:
1/2 cup sugar
1/4 cup water
Dash of salt
3 large egg whites (at room
  temperature)
1/2 teaspoon cream of tartar
1/4 teaspoon vanilla extract

1. To prepare cupcakes, place coconut milk, ¼ cup coconut, and vanilla bean in a small saucepan; bring to a boil over medium-high heat. Remove pan from heat. Cover and let stand until room temperature, about 20 minutes. Remove and discard vanilla bean.

2. Preheat oven to 350°.

3. Place remaining 3 tablespoons coconut on a baking sheet. Bake at 350° for 5 to 6 minutes or until lightly toasted, stirring after 4 minutes. Set aside.

4. Weigh or lightly spoon flour into dry measuring cups; level with a knife. Combine flour and next 3 ingredients in a bowl; stir with a whisk. Place sugar, butter, and oil in a large bowl. Beat with a mixer at medium speed until light and fluffy, about 3 minutes. Stir in cooled coconut milk mixture. Add flour mixture; beat at low speed until just combined.

5. Place 3 egg whites and ½ teaspoon cream of tartar in a large bowl. Using clean, dry beaters, beat egg white mixture at medium speed until foamy; beat at high speed until soft peaks form, about 2 minutes. Gently fold one-fourth of egg white mixture into batter; gently fold in remaining egg white mixture. Divide batter among 12 muffin cups lined with cupcake liners. Bake at 350° for 17 to 18 minutes or until a wooden pick inserted in center comes out clean. Cool 5 minutes in pans on a wire rack; remove from pans. Cool completely on wire rack.

6. To prepare icing, combine ½ cup sugar, ¼ cup water, and salt in a saucepan; bring to a boil, stirring just until sugar dissolves. Cook, without stirring, until a candy thermometer registers 230°. Place 3 egg whites and ½ teaspoon cream of tartar in a large bowl; beat with clean, dry beaters at medium speed until foamy. Beat at high speed until medium peaks form. With mixer at low speed, pour hot syrup in a thin stream down the side of mixing bowl. Gradually increase speed to high; beat 3 minutes or until thickened and cooled. Beat in vanilla. Mound about 2 tablespoons icing on top of each cupcake. Sprinkle cupcakes with reserved toasted coconut.

SERVES 12 (serving size: 1 cupcake)
CALORIES 244; FAT 9.9g (sat 5.2g, mono 3g, poly 1g); PROTEIN 4g; CARB 36g; FIBER 1g; CHOL 15mg; IRON 1mg; SODIUM 196mg; CALC 28mg

TECHNIQUE TIP

What's the difference between muffins and cupcakes? Muffin batters are thicker, stirred less, and many have fruit, nuts, or both added, making them heartier. They also have less sugar and fat, resulting in a crumb (or texture) that is denser than cupcakes. Cupcake batters are thinner, with more sugar and fat added, resulting in a soft, silky texture and melt-in-your-mouth goodness.

PUMPKIN CREAM MUFFINS

Hands-on: 20 min. Total: 60 min.

Combining pumpkin bread and cheesecake, these rich cream-filled muffins represent the best of fall flavors. Alternating the pumpkin batter with the cream cheese filling assures an evenly baked muffin with a creamy center.

Baking spray with flour
4 ounces ⅓-less-fat cream cheese, softened
3 tablespoons powdered sugar
1¼ teaspoons vanilla extract, divided
6.75 ounces all-purpose flour (about 1½ cups)
2 teaspoons baking powder
1½ teaspoons ground cinnamon
¾ teaspoon ground ginger
¾ teaspoon ground allspice
½ teaspoon salt
¼ teaspoon baking soda
¼ teaspoon ground cloves
¾ cup granulated sugar
¼ cup unsalted butter
2 large eggs
1 cup canned pumpkin puree
¼ cup chopped pecans

1. Preheat oven to 425°. Place 12 muffin cup liners in muffin cups; coat liners lightly with baking spray.

2. Place cream cheese, powdered sugar, and ¼ teaspoon vanilla in a small bowl; stir until smooth. Set aside.

3. Weigh or lightly spoon flour into dry measuring cups; level with a knife. Combine flour and next 7 ingredients (through cloves) in a bowl, stirring with a whisk.

4. Place 1 teaspoon vanilla, granulated sugar, and butter in a bowl; beat with a mixer at medium speed until well combined, about 3 minutes. Add eggs, 1 at a time, beating well after each addition. Add pumpkin; beat at low speed until combined. Add flour mixture; beat at low speed 1 minute or until just combined.

5. Spoon batter into prepared muffin cups, filling one-third full. Top each with about 2 teaspoons cream cheese mixture; divide remaining batter evenly over cream cheese mixture. Sprinkle nuts evenly over batter. Bake at 425° for 5 minutes. Reduce oven temperature to 375°. Bake muffins at 375° for an additional 10 minutes or until muffins spring back when touched lightly in center. Remove muffins from pan, and cool on a wire rack.

SERVES 12 (serving size: 1 muffin)
CALORIES 210; FAT 8.7g (sat 4.1g, mono 2.8g, poly 1g); PROTEIN 4g; CARB 30g; FIBER 2g; CHOL 48mg; IRON 1mg; SODIUM 250mg; CALC 74mg

RASPBERRY AND ALMOND LINZER MUFFINS

Hands-on: 20 min. Total: 60 min.

Classic Linzer Torte is rich almond pastry surrounding raspberry jam. These lightened, quick, and easy muffins are an equally satisfying version of the old-world dessert.

Baking spray with flour
½ cup almond flour
6.75 ounces all-purpose flour
  (about 1½ cups)
2 teaspoons baking powder
½ teaspoon salt
¼ teaspoon baking soda
2 ounces almond paste
½ cup sugar
¼ cup butter, softened
½ teaspoon vanilla extract
2 large eggs
⅔ cup 2% reduced-fat milk
¼ cup raspberry jam
¼ cup sliced almonds

1. Preheat oven to 350°. Place 12 muffin cup liners in muffin cups; coat liners lightly with baking spray.

2. Sprinkle almond flour on a baking sheet. Bake at 350° for 6 minutes or until beginning to brown and become fragrant, stirring after 3 minutes. Cool to room temperature. Increase oven temperature to 425°.

3. Weigh or lightly spoon flour into dry measuring cups; level with a knife. Combine flours and next 3 ingredients (through baking soda) in a bowl, stirring with a whisk.

4. Crumble almond paste into a large bowl; add sugar. Beat with a mixer at medium-low speed until mixture becomes sandy, about 3 minutes. Add butter and vanilla; beat 2 minutes or until well combined. Add eggs, 1 at a time, beating well after each addition. Add flour mixture and milk alternately to butter mixture, beginning and ending with flour mixture.

5. Spoon batter into prepared muffin cups, filling one-third full. Top each with about 1 teaspoon jam; top with remaining batter. Sprinkle nuts evenly over batter. Bake at 425° for 5 minutes. Reduce oven temperature to 375°. Bake at 375° for an additional 10 minutes or until muffins spring back when touched lightly in center. Remove muffins from pan immediately, and cool on a wire rack.

SERVES 12 (serving size: 1 muffin)

CALORIES 221; FAT 9.8g (sat 3.2g, mono 4.3g, poly 1.5g); PROTEIN 5g; CARB 29g; FIBER 1g; CHOL 42mg; IRON 1mg; SODIUM 226mg; CALC 91mg

ALMOND PASTE

Almond paste adds intense almond flavor and additional sweetness to these muffins. The paste is a concentrated mix of finely ground almonds and sugar. Using just a small amount can boost almond flavor in baked goods without adding excessive calories.

1. Baking bacon is a lot less messy than cooking it in a skillet. Line a baking sheet with foil to minimize the mess, and then place a wire rack on the pan.

2. Coat both sides of the bacon with the spice mixture, and place on rack, leaving a little room around each slice so the heat can circulate.

3. Place the pan in the oven, and then heat the oven to 400°. By beginning the cooking process in a cold oven, the bacon won't curl up.

SPICY BACON AND BREW "MANFFINS"

Hands-on: 22 min. Total: 50 min.

Bacon, dark beer, and hot pepper aren't the standard mix-ins for muffins, but these savory "manffins" will particularly appeal to the guys in your family. Not a beer fan? No problem. Substitute an equal amount of reduced-fat milk for the beer.

3 tablespoons dark brown sugar
2 teaspoons ground red pepper
2 teaspoons water
3 applewood-smoked bacon slices
Cooking spray
3 tablespoons old-fashioned rolled oats
1 tablespoon all-purpose flour
1 tablespoon unsalted butter, melted
7.9 ounces all-purpose flour (about 1¾ cups)
½ cup packed dark brown sugar
2 teaspoons baking powder
¼ teaspoon salt
¼ teaspoon baking soda
⅔ cup Guinness beer, at room temperature
3 tablespoons canola oil
1 teaspoon vanilla extract
1 large egg

1. Combine 3 tablespoons brown sugar, pepper, and 2 teaspoons water in a small bowl, stirring until smooth. Spread sugar mixture evenly over both sides of bacon. Place bacon on a wire rack coated with cooking spray; place rack in a baking sheet lined with foil. Place baking sheet in cold oven. Preheat oven to 400°, and cook bacon 18 minutes or until crisp. Cool; finely chop bacon.

2. Combine oats and 1 tablespoon flour in a small bowl. Add butter and 2 tablespoons chopped bacon, stirring until combined but still crumbly. Set streusel aside.

3. Reduce oven temperature to 350°. Place 12 muffin liners in muffin cups.

4. Weigh or lightly spoon flour into dry measuring cups; level with a knife. Combine flour, remaining chopped bacon, ½ cup brown sugar, baking powder, salt, and baking soda in a large bowl, stirring with a whisk. Combine beer, oil, vanilla, and egg in a bowl; gently stir with a whisk until combined. Add beer mixture to flour mixture, stirring until just combined. Spoon batter into prepared muffin cups. Sprinkle streusel evenly over tops.

5. Bake at 350° for 16 to 18 minutes or until a wooden pick inserted in center comes out clean. Cool 5 minutes in pan. Remove from pan, and serve warm or at room temperature.

SERVES 12 (serving size: 1 muffin)
CALORIES 177; FAT 5.8g (sat 1.3g, mono 2.7g, poly 1.2g); PROTEIN 3g; CARB 27g; FIBER 1g; CHOL 20mg; IRON 1mg; SODIUM 202mg; CALC 51mg

UPPER CRUST

STRAWBERRY-RHUBARB PIE

Hands-on: 30 min. Total: 3 hr. 15 min.

6.75 ounces all-purpose flour
  (about 1½ cups)
¼ teaspoon salt
¼ teaspoon baking powder
3 tablespoons unsalted butter,
  chilled
2 tablespoons natural
  shortening (such as Earth
  Balance), chilled
¼ cup ice water
1½ teaspoons white vinegar
Baking spray with flour

3 cups halved fresh strawberries
  (or quartered if large)
1½ cups chopped rhubarb
  (fresh or frozen, thawed)
1 cup granulated sugar
¼ cup cornstarch
2 tablespoons unsalted butter,
  melted
1 teaspoon ground cardamom
1 teaspoon vanilla extract
⅛ teaspoon salt
1 large egg white, lightly beaten
2 teaspoons turbinado sugar

1. Weigh or lightly spoon flour into dry measuring cups; level with a knife. Place flour, salt, and baking powder in a food processor; process to combine. Cut butter and shortening into ½-inch pieces. Add butter and shortening to bowl; pulse 3 times or until butter is about the size of dried peas. Sprinkle ice water and vinegar over mixture; pulse 3 to 4 times or until mixture looks sandy. Pour mixture onto a lightly floured work surface; gather mixture together, and press into a ball. Divide into 2 pieces (1 piece measuring two-thirds of dough and the other remaining one-third of dough). Cover each with plastic wrap; press into a disc. Chill 30 minutes.

2. Preheat oven to 350°.

3. Unwrap largest dough disc, and place on a lightly floured work surface. Roll to an 11-inch circle. Place into a 9-inch pie plate lightly coated with baking spray. Fold edges under, and flute decoratively. Unwrap smaller dough disc and place on a lightly floured work surface. Roll to ¼-inch thickness. Cut as many 1½-inch decorative shapes as possible using a floured cookie cutter, rerolling scraps only 1 time.

4. Place strawberries and next 7 ingredients in a large bowl; toss gently to combine. Pour filling into prepared pie plate. Arrange cut-outs on top of filling. Brush edge of crust and cutouts with egg white; sprinkle top of pie with turbinado sugar for sparkle and crunch. Bake at 350° for 55 minutes or until golden and bubbly. Shield edges of pie with foil if getting too brown. Place pie on a wire rack; cool completely before slicing.

SERVES 10 (serving size: 1 slice)
CALORIES 261; FAT 8.9g (sat 4.7g, mono 2.5g, poly 1g); PROTEIN 3g;
CARB 43g; FIBER 2g; CHOL 15mg; IRON 1mg; SODIUM 108mg; CALC 36mg

WORKING WITH PIECRUST

1. Folding the edges of the pie dough under gives it a thicker edge. It's also an opportunity to add a little decorative touch, like crimping or fluting.

2. The cutouts are just fun! You can make them into any shape you like, using any shape cookie cutter you have. Place the cutouts as you like—clustered on one side, in rows, or over the entire surface of the pie.

3. Brush the tops of the cutouts lightly with beaten egg white and sprinkle with sugar for a glistening and sparkly finish.

DOUBLE CRUST APPLE PIE

Hands-on: 41 min. Total: 2 hr. 26 min.

A double crust seals in all the apples' natural juices as the pie bakes, making for full-on apple flavor and lots of juicy, tender bits of apple. Tossing the apple slices with apple juice prevents them from browning as you peel and slice them, and it adds an additional boost of apple flavor. Use a variety of apples for a more interesting texture: Golden Delicious for melt-in-your mouth tenderness, Granny Smith for a little tartness, and Honey Crisp for sweetness.

CRUST:
10.1 ounces all-purpose flour
   (about 2¼ cups)
½ teaspoon baking powder
⅜ teaspoon salt
3 tablespoons unsalted butter,
   chilled
3 tablespoons natural shortening
   (such as Earth Balance), chilled
6 tablespoons ice water
2 teaspoons white vinegar

FILLING:
6 cups (⅛-inch-thick) slices
   peeled apple

¼ cup unsweetened apple juice
¼ cup packed brown sugar
2 tablespoons all-purpose flour
1 tablespoon cornstarch
½ teaspoon ground cinnamon
¼ teaspoon freshly ground
   nutmeg
¼ teaspoon salt
Baking spray with flour
2 tablespoons unsalted butter,
   diced
1 large egg white, lightly beaten
2 teaspoons granulated sugar

1. To prepare crust, weigh or lightly spoon flour into dry measuring cups; level with a knife. Place flour, baking powder, and salt in a food processor; process to combine. Cut chilled butter and shortening into ½-inch pieces; add to bowl. Pulse 2 to 3 times or until butter is about the size of dried peas. Sprinkle ice water and vinegar over mixture. Pulse 2 to 3 times or until mixture is combined and looks like coarse sand.

2. Scrape mixture onto a lightly floured work surface. Press mixture into a ball; divide into 2 equal pieces. Press each half into a 4-inch disc. Cover each disc with plastic wrap, and chill 30 minutes. (The dough can be made 1 day ahead. If it's chilled for 24 hours, let it stand at room temperature for 10 minutes before rolling.)

3. Preheat oven to 425°.

4. To prepare filling, place apples and juice in a large bowl; toss to coat. Stir together brown sugar and next 5 ingredients (through salt) in a small bowl. Sprinkle apples with brown sugar mixture; toss well to combine.

5. Unwrap 1 dough disc, and place on a lightly floured work surface. Roll to an 11-inch circle. Place into a 9-inch pie plate lightly coated with baking spray. Pour filling into prepared pie plate (the pan will be very full). Arrange diced butter on top of filling. Roll remaining half of dough into a 10-inch circle on a lightly floured surface. Place dough on top of pie; fold edges under, and flute decoratively. Cut slits in top of dough to allow steam to escape. Lightly brush top of dough with egg white. Sprinkle with granulated sugar.

6. Bake at 425° for 15 minutes; reduce oven temperature to 350°. Bake an additional 1 hour or until golden and bubbly. Shield edges of pie with foil if getting too brown. Place pie on a wire rack; cool completely before slicing.

SERVES 10 (serving size: 1 slice)
CALORIES 264; FAT 10.4g (sat 5.2g, mono 3g, poly 1.3g); PROTEIN 4g; CARB 39g; FIBER 2g; CHOL 15mg; IRON 2mg; SODIUM 178mg; CALC 30mg

1. Use a fluted pastry wheel to cut the dough into strips. You can use a knife or pizza cutter, but the pastry wheel gives it a pretty edge.

2. Place 5 strips of pastry across the filling; rotate the pie so that the strips are vertical. From left to right, number the strips 1 through 5. Fold strips 2 and 4 back, leaving about 1 inch; place one strip of pastry across the pie horizontally; unfold strips 2 and 4.

3. Fold strips 1, 3, and 5 back, leaving about 3 inches; place one strip of pastry; unfold strips 1, 3, and 5. Fold strips 2 and 4 back to center of pie; place one strip of pastry; unfold strips 2 and 4. Repeat process with remaining 2 strips of pastry.

CRANBERRY-RASPBERRY PIE

Hands-on: 40 min. Total: 1 hr. 55 min.

6.75 ounces all-purpose flour (about 1½ cups)
½ teaspoon salt, divided
¼ teaspoon baking powder
3 tablespoons unsalted butter, chilled
3 tablespoons natural shortening (such as Earth Balance), chilled
4 tablespoons ice water
1½ teaspoons white vinegar
Baking spray with flour
1 (8-ounce) package fresh cranberries (about 2 cups)
1 cup (½-inch) diced apple
1 tablespoon fresh lemon juice
½ cup granulated sugar
¼ cup cornstarch
3 (6-ounce) packages fresh raspberries, divided
2 tablespoons unsalted butter, diced
1 large egg white, lightly beaten
1 tablespoon turbinado sugar

1. Weigh or lightly spoon flour into dry measuring cups; level with a knife. Place flour, ¼ teaspoon salt, and baking powder in a food processor; process to combine. Cut butter and shortening into ½-inch pieces, and add to bowl. Pulse 3 times or until butter is about the size of dried peas. Sprinkle ice water and vinegar over mixture; pulse 3 to 4 times or until mixture looks sandy. Pour mixture onto a lightly floured work surface; gather mixture together, and press into a ball. Divide into 2 pieces (measuring two-thirds and one-third of dough); gently press into 4-inch discs, and cover with plastic wrap. Chill 30 minutes.

2. Preheat oven to 350°.

3. Unwrap the largest dough disc, and place on a lightly floured work surface. Roll to an 11-inch circle. Place into a 9-inch pie plate lightly coated with baking spray. Fold edges under, and flute decoratively.

4. Combine cranberries, apple, and juice. Sprinkle with granulated sugar, cornstarch, and ¼ teaspoon salt; toss well. Add 2 packages raspberries; toss gently. Spoon mixture into prepared pie plate. Arrange remaining package of raspberries over cranberry mixture. Dot pie with diced butter.

5. Unwrap smaller dough disc; place on a lightly floured work surface. Roll to a 10 x 5–inch rectangle. Cut lengthwise into 10 (½-inch) strips and arrange in a lattice over raspberries. Seal strips to edge of crust. Brush lattice and edge of pie with egg white. Sprinkle with turbinado sugar. Bake at 350° for 45 minutes or until golden and bubbly. Shield edges of pie with foil if getting too brown. Place pie on a wire rack; cool completely on wire rack before slicing.

SERVES 10 (serving size: 1 slice)
CALORIES 261; FAT 10.6g (sat 5.2g, mono 3.1g, poly 1.4g); PROTEIN 3g;
CARB 39g; FIBER 5g; CHOL 15mg; IRON 1mg; SODIUM 137mg; CALC 27mg

LEMON SHAKER PIE

Hands-on: 35 min. Total: 5 hr.

Using the whole lemon is part of the classic Shaker lemon pie. I'm not as hearty as the Shakers, so I macerate them in a sugar mixture for 3 hours (or up to overnight), which tenderizes the rind and minimizes the bitterness of the pith. Use a mandoline to make thin, even lemon slices. And don't worry too much about getting all the seeds out at first; after the lemons and sugar mixture stand, the rest of the seeds will float to the top so you can easily scoop them out.

LEMONS AND SYRUP:
2 medium lemons
⅔ cup granulated sugar
½ cup golden cane syrup
(such as Lyle's Golden Syrup)
⅛ teaspoon salt

CRUST:
5.6 ounces all-purpose flour
(about 1¼ cups)
¼ teaspoon baking powder
¼ teaspoon salt
2 tablespoons unsalted butter, chilled

2 tablespoons natural shortening
(such as Earth Balance), chilled
3 tablespoons ice water
1 teaspoon white vinegar
Baking spray with flour

FILLING AND FINISHING:
2 tablespoons unsalted butter, melted
2 tablespoons all-purpose flour
4 large eggs, well beaten
1 large egg white, lightly beaten
1 tablespoon turbinado sugar

1. To prepare lemons and syrup, remove about ½ inch of each end of the lemons; discard. Slice lemons crosswise as thin as possible. Discard seeds. Combine granulated sugar, cane syrup, and salt in a medium bowl. Add lemons; toss to coat. Cover and let stand at room temperature at least 3 hours or up to overnight.

2. To prepare crust, weigh or lightly spoon flour into dry measuring cups; level with a knife. Place flour, baking powder, and salt in a food processor; process to combine. Cut chilled butter and shortening into ½-inch pieces; add to processor. Pulse 2 to 3 times or until butter is about the size of dried peas. Sprinkle ice water and vinegar over mixture. Pulse 2 to 3 times or until mixture is combined and looks like coarse sand. (Do not overprocess the mixture or it will become clumpy and tough.)

3. Scrape dough onto a lightly floured work surface; gather mixture together, and press into a 4-inch disc. Wrap disc with plastic wrap, and chill 30 minutes. (The dough can be made 1 day ahead. If it's chilled for 24 hours, let it stand at room temperature for 10 minutes before rolling.)

4. Preheat oven to 400°.

5. Unwrap dough, and place on a lightly floured work surface. Roll into an 11-inch circle. Place into a 9-inch pie plate lightly coated with baking spray. Fold edges under, and flute decoratively.

6. To prepare filling, remove lemons from cane syrup mixture, reserving cane syrup mixture; set lemons aside. Combine melted butter and 2 tablespoons flour in a medium bowl, stirring with a whisk until smooth. Add eggs to flour mixture, stirring to combine. Add reserved cane syrup mixture to flour mixture, stirring with a whisk until smooth. Arrange half of reserved lemon slices in bottom of piecrust. Pour cane syrup mixture over lemons. Arrange remaining lemon slices over the top.

7. To finish pie, brush edge of pie with egg white, and sprinkle with turbinado sugar. Bake at 400° for 25 minutes. Reduce oven temperature to 350° (do not remove pie from oven); bake an additional 10 minutes or until filling begins to just set in the middle. Shield edges of pie with foil if getting too brown. Place pie on a wire rack; cool completely before slicing.

SERVES 10 (serving size: 1 slice)
CALORIES 269; FAT 9.5g (sat 4.6g, mono 2.9g, poly 1.2g); PROTEIN 5g;
CARB 43g; FIBER 1g; CHOL 87mg; IRON 1mg; SODIUM 186mg; CALC 27mg

WALNUT-CHOCOLATE PIE
WITH RICH PASTRY CRUST

Hands-on: 18 min. Total: 1 hr. 33 min.

The rich pastry crust is like a soft sugar cookie but less sweet.

5.6 ounces all-purpose flour
 (about 1¼ cups)
½ cup powdered sugar
¼ teaspoon salt
3 tablespoons unsalted butter,
 chilled and diced
2 large eggs, separated and
 divided
Baking spray with flour
½ cup light-colored corn syrup
⅓ cup packed dark brown sugar

1 tablespoon unsalted butter,
 melted
1 teaspoon vanilla extract
⅛ teaspoon salt
2 large eggs, lightly beaten
2 large egg whites, lightly beaten
⅔ cup lightly toasted chopped
 walnuts
1½ ounces bittersweet
 chocolate, finely chopped
 and melted

TECHNIQUE TIP
When a recipe calls for just a little bit of melted chocolate, I like to melt it in the microwave. Finely chop the chocolate, and place it in a microwave-safe dish. Microwave at HIGH, stirring every 15 seconds, until it's completely melted and smooth.

1. Weigh or lightly spoon flour into dry measuring cups; level with a knife. Place flour, powdered sugar, and salt in a food processor; pulse 3 to 4 times to combine. Add chilled butter; pulse 3 to 4 times or until mixture looks sandy. Add 1 whole egg and 1 egg yolk; pulse 5 to 6 times or until mixture begins to clump together. Scrape mixture onto a lightly floured work surface. Gather mixture together, and press into a disc. Cover with plastic wrap, and chill 30 minutes.

2. Preheat oven to 375°.

3. Unwrap dough, and place on a lightly floured work surface. Roll dough into an 11-inch circle. Place dough into a 9-inch pie plate lightly coated with baking spray. Press dough against bottom and sides of pan. Fold edges under, and flute decoratively. Line bottom of dough with parchment paper; arrange pie weights or dried beans on parchment paper. Bake at 375° for 10 minutes. Remove from oven; remove pie weights and parchment paper. Brush pie dough with lightly beaten remaining egg white. Bake an additional 5 minutes to set egg wash. Reduce oven temperature to 350°.

4. Combine corn syrup and next 6 ingredients (through egg whites) in a bowl, stirring well. Stir in walnuts and melted chocolate. Pour mixture into prepared crust. Bake at 350° for 25 minutes or until center is almost set. Shield edges with foil if getting too brown. Cool completely on a wire rack before slicing.

SERVES 10 (serving size: 1 slice)
CALORIES 300; FAT 13.4g (sat 5g, mono 2.6g, poly 4.3g); PROTEIN 6g;
CARB 42g; FIBER 1g; CHOL 87mg; IRON 2mg; SODIUM 141mg; CALC 34mg

MY TOP 5 TIPS FOR
MAKING LIGHT PIECRUSTS

I'll be honest here: Developing a from-scratch crust that is lower in calories and saturated fat while still having a wonderful buttery taste and flaky texture is a tall order. But through lots of trial and error, I've found a way to deliver just that. Here are my top tips for creating delicious piecrusts.

1 *Make sure your butter (and/or shortening) is refrigerator cold—35° to 38°. (You can stick the butter in the freezer for 20 to 30 minutes to make sure it's really cold.) Why? Cold butter doesn't mix as well with the flour and other dry ingredients, which is exactly what you want. When the crust goes into the oven, those little pockets of cold butter heat up and produce steam, creating those yummy flaky layers.*

2 *My secret weapon: Earth Balance Natural Shortening sticks, which have a third less saturated fat than butter without the hydrogenated oils. Commercially prepared shortening is filled with teeny-tiny air bubbles that create flaky layers in the crust, so combining the two gives the best possible flavor and flakiness. You can find Earth Balance Natural Shortening sticks in the refrigerated section of most grocery stores.*

3 *Using ice water to make the piecrust provides an extra bit of insurance—it helps keep the butter cold. Put three to four ice cubes in a coffee cup with water, and then measure out what you need from the cup, 1 tablespoon at a time.*

4 *Vinegar helps prevent gluten from forming, creating a tender crust. While it is evaporating as it cooks in the oven, it leaves flaky layers in its wake. Use the mildest vinegar you can find, like white distilled vinegar. Vodka also works in the same way vinegar does.*

5 *When rolling out the dough, work quickly. The goal is for the fat (the butter or shortening) to remain as cold as possible before the piecrust goes in the oven. Spending too much time handling the dough will warm the butter up, and it will melt and act like glue instead of steam, leaving you with a crust that's greasy and tough. Use only a minimal amount of flour on your work surface when rolling out the dough—the more flour incorporated into the dough, the tougher and drier it will be.*

SILKY SWEET POTATO–PECAN PIE

Hands-on: 22 min. Total: 2 hr. 55 min.

1 (1-pound) sweet potato
5.6 ounces all-purpose flour (about 1¼ cups)
½ cup powdered sugar
⅛ teaspoon salt
3 tablespoons unsalted butter, chilled and diced
2 large eggs, separated and divided
Baking spray with flour
1 cup whole milk
½ cup granulated sugar

2 tablespoons unsalted butter, melted
1 teaspoon vanilla extract
¾ teaspoon ground cinnamon
½ teaspoon ground allspice
¼ teaspoon salt
2 large eggs
2 large egg whites
⅓ cup chopped pecans
1½ cups frozen fat-free whipped topping (such as Cool Whip), thawed

1. Preheat oven to 400°.

2. Wrap sweet potato in foil; bake at 400° for 1 hour or until tender. Cool completely. Peel.

3. Weigh or lightly spoon flour into dry measuring cups; level with a knife. Place flour, powdered sugar, and salt in a food processor; pulse 3 to 4 times to combine. Add chilled butter; pulse 3 to 4 times or until mixture looks sandy. Add 1 whole egg and 1 egg yolk; pulse 5 to 6 times or until mixture begins to clump together. Scrape mixture onto a lightly floured work surface. Gather mixture together, and press into a disc. Cover with plastic wrap, and chill 30 minutes.

4. Preheat oven to 350°.

5. Unwrap dough, and place on a lightly floured work surface. Roll into an 11-inch circle. Fit dough into a 9-inch pie plate lightly coated with baking spray. Press dough against bottom and sides of pan. Fold edges under, and flute decoratively. Brush dough with lightly beaten remaining egg white. Place pan in refrigerator to chill while preparing filling.

6. Place peeled sweet potato, milk, and next 8 ingredients (through egg whites) in a food processor; process until smooth. Pour mixture into prepared pie plate. Sprinkle nuts around edge of filling. Bake at 350° for 45 minutes or until almost set in the center. Shield edges of pie with foil if getting too brown. Cool completely on a wire rack before slicing. Top with whipped topping.

SERVES 10 (serving size: 1 slice and about 2½ tablespoons whipped topping)
CALORIES 300; FAT 11.3g (sat 5g, mono 3.9g, poly 1.5g); PROTEIN 7g;
CARB 43g; FIBER 2g; CHOL 92mg; IRON 2mg; SODIUM 161mg; CALC 65mg

TECHNIQUE TIP

Using a food processor to combine the filling ingredients breaks down the sweet potato's stringy fibers, making this pie silky smooth.

KEY LIME CURD PIE

Hands-on: 32 min. Total: 3 hr. 50 min.

Key lime pie can have a rubbery texture or be overly tart, but this creamy curd version is light and satisfying with just the right amount of tartness.

CRUST:
10 graham cracker sheets (about 6 ounces)
3 tablespoons brown sugar
1/8 teaspoon salt
1 large egg, separated
1 tablespoon unsalted butter, melted
Baking spray with flour

FILLING:
1 cup granulated sugar, divided
1 cup whole milk

1/3 cup Key lime juice (about 3/4 pound fresh Key limes)
1 1/2 tablespoons cornstarch
1/4 teaspoon salt
3 large eggs
2 tablespoons unsalted butter
1 cup frozen reduced-calorie whipped topping (such as Cool Whip), thawed
1 teaspoon freshly grated Key lime rind

1. Preheat oven to 350°.

2. To prepare crust, place crackers, brown sugar, and 1/8 teaspoon salt in a food processor; process until finely ground. Place egg white in a small bowl; stir with a whisk until foamy. Place egg yolk in a large bowl; set aside. Add egg white and melted butter to food processor; pulse 3 to 4 times or until crumbs are moist (do not overprocess). Press crumb mixture into the bottom and up the sides of a 9-inch pie plate lightly coated with baking spray. Bake at 350° for 12 minutes or until lightly browned. Cool completely on a wire rack.

3. To prepare filling, place 2/3 cup sugar and milk in a medium saucepan over medium heat; bring to a simmer, stirring occasionally. Add 1/3 cup sugar, juice, cornstarch, 1/4 teaspoon salt, and eggs to the large bowl containing the egg yolk; stir well with a whisk to dissolve cornstarch. Gradually pour hot milk mixture into egg mixture, stirring constantly with a whisk. Return milk mixture to pan. Cook over medium heat until thick and bubbly, about 5 minutes, stirring constantly. Remove pan from heat. Add 2 tablespoons butter, stirring until combined.

4. Place pan in a large ice-filled bowl for 10 minutes or until mixture reaches room temperature, stirring occasionally. Spoon filling into prepared crust; cover with plastic wrap. Chill 3 hours or until set. To serve, top pie with whipped topping, and sprinkle with lime rind.

SERVES 8 (serving size: 1 slice and 2 tablespoons whipped topping)
CALORIES 300; FAT 10.3g (sat 5.3g, mono 2.9g, poly 1.3g); PROTEIN 5g;
CARB 49g; FIBER 0g; CHOL 108mg; IRON 1mg; SODIUM 199mg; CALC 58mg

KEY LIMES

Tiny Key limes are very tart and just a little bit on the bitter side but so remarkable in a creamy curd pie like this. Use fresh Key limes if possible and be sure to grate some of the rind for decorating the top of the pie. Shelf-stable Key lime juice is an acceptable substitute for fresh Key limes. If Key limes or Key lime juice are impossible to find, substitute an equal amount of regular fresh lime juice for the Key lime juice.

LEMON CREAM PIE

Hands-on: 20 min. Total: 3 hr. 30 min.

It's amazing how just a touch of cream cheese—even the ⅓-less-fat variety—adds richness and creaminess to this lemon filling. It's surrounded by a vanilla wafer cookie crumb crust—that doesn't hurt, either.

CRUST:
1¼ cups reduced-fat vanilla wafer cookie crumbs (about 40 cookies)
2 teaspoons cornstarch
⅛ teaspoon salt
1 tablespoon unsalted butter, melted
1 large egg white
Baking spray with flour

FILLING:
⅔ cup sugar
4 teaspoons grated lemon rind, divided
¼ cup fresh lemon juice
3 tablespoons cornstarch
⅛ teaspoon salt
3 large eggs
1½ cups 2% reduced-fat milk
2 ounces ⅓-less-fat cream cheese
2 tablespoons unsalted butter
1 cup frozen fat-free whipped topping (such as Cool Whip), thawed

1. Preheat oven to 350°.

2. To prepare crust, place cookie crumbs, cornstarch, and salt in a food processor; process until finely ground. Add butter and egg white; pulse 3 to 4 times or until mixture is well combined and moist (do not overprocess). Press mixture into the bottom and up the sides of a 9-inch pie plate lightly coated with baking spray. Bake at 350° for 12 minutes or until crisp and golden. Cool completely on a wire rack.

3. To prepare filling, combine sugar, 1 tablespoon rind, and next 4 ingredients (through eggs) in a large bowl, stirring well. Combine milk and cream cheese in a saucepan over medium heat; stir until smooth. Cook until mixture reaches 180° or until tiny bubbles form around edge (about 8 minutes), stirring constantly. Gradually add hot milk mixture to sugar mixture, stirring constantly with a whisk. Return milk mixture to pan, and cook over medium heat until thick and bubbly, stirring constantly. Remove from heat; add butter, stirring until butter melts.

4. Place pan in a large ice-filled bowl for 10 minutes or until mixture is room temperature, stirring occasionally. Spoon filling into prepared crust; cover surface with plastic wrap. Chill 3 hours or until set. To serve, dollop 1 tablespoon whipped topping on each slice, and sprinkle with 1 teaspoon lemon rind.

SERVES 8 (serving size: 1 slice)
CALORIES 259; FAT 10.6g (sat 5.3g, mono 3.3g, poly 1.1g); PROTEIN 6g; CARB 36g; FIBER 0g; CHOL 96mg; IRON 1mg; SODIUM 206mg; CALC 83mg

TECHNIQUE TIP

Cookie crumbs and graham crackers make a wonderful crust for cream pies. However, because of the amount of saturated fat in butter, I often use egg whites to hold the cookie crumbs together. But using all egg whites can result in a crust that isn't very crisp. Adding cornstarch to the crust soaks up extra moisture and helps give the crust the perfect crisp texture.

BRANDY-PUMPKIN CREAM PIE

Hands-on: 40 min. Total: 4 hr. 30 min.

How about an adult version of pumpkin pie? This is it. Adding just a touch of brandy elevates the tried-and-true flavor of pumpkin pie and all its traditional spices. Feel free to omit the brandy, if you prefer. There's no need to replace it with any other liquid. The rich pastry dough is like sugar cookie dough, just less sweet and a little sturdier to support the filling.

CRUST:
5.6 ounces all-purpose flour
   (about 1¼ cups)
½ cup powdered sugar
¼ teaspoon salt
3 tablespoons unsalted butter,
   chilled and diced
2 large eggs, separated and
   divided
Baking spray with flour

FILLING:
¾ cup granulated sugar, divided
1 cup canned pumpkin puree
¼ cup cornstarch

1 teaspoon ground cinnamon
½ teaspoon ground allspice
½ teaspoon ground ginger
¼ teaspoon salt
⅛ teaspoon ground cloves
2 large eggs
1½ cups whole milk
2 tablespoons brandy
2 tablespoons unsalted butter,
   softened
1 teaspoon vanilla extract
1½ cups frozen fat-free whipped
   topping (such as Cool Whip),
   thawed

1. To prepare crust, weigh or lightly spoon flour into dry measuring cups; level with a knife. Place flour, powdered sugar, and salt in a food processor; pulse 3 to 4 times to combine. Add butter; pulse 3 to 4 times or until mixture looks sandy. Add 1 whole egg and 1 egg yolk; pulse 5 to 6 times or until mixture begins to clump together. Scrape mixture onto a lightly floured work surface. Gather mixture together, and press into a disc. Cover with plastic wrap, and chill 30 minutes.

2. Preheat oven to 375°.

3. Unwrap dough, and place on a lightly floured work surface. Roll into an 11-inch circle. Fit dough into a 9-inch pie plate lightly coated with baking spray. Press dough against bottom and sides of pan. Fold edges under, and flute decoratively. Line bottom of dough with parchment paper; arrange pie weights or dried beans on parchment paper. Bake at 375° for 15 minutes. Remove from oven; remove pie weights and parchment paper. Brush pie dough with lightly beaten remaining egg white. Bake at 375° for an additional 15 minutes or until golden brown. Shield edges of pie with foil if getting too brown. Cool completely on a wire rack.

4. To prepare filling, combine ¼ cup sugar and next 8 ingredients (through eggs) in a large bowl; stir well with a whisk.

5. Heat milk and ½ cup sugar in a medium, heavy saucepan over medium-high heat to 180° or until tiny bubbles form around edge (do not boil). Gradually add hot milk mixture to pumpkin mixture, stirring constantly with a whisk. Return milk mixture to pan; cook over medium heat until thick and bubbly, about 8 minutes, stirring constantly. Remove from heat; add brandy, butter, and vanilla, stirring until combined.

6. Place pan in a large ice-filled bowl for 10 minutes or until filling reaches room temperature, stirring occasionally. Spoon into prepared crust; cover surface of filling with plastic wrap. Chill 3 hours or until set. Top each serving with whipped topping.

SERVES 10 (serving size: 1 slice and about 2½ tablespoons whipped topping)
CALORIES 289; FAT 9.1g (sat 5g, mono 2.5g, poly 0.7g); PROTEIN 6g; CARB 44g;
FIBER 2g; CHOL 93mg; IRON 1mg; SODIUM 169mg; CALC 65mg

CHAI CREAM PIE

Hands-on: 35 min. Total: 4 hr. 15 min.

This spice-rich pie is aromatic and creamy smooth. Adding cornstarch to the graham cracker crust helps keep it crisp, which is a lovely contrast to the filling.

9 sheets reduced-fat cinnamon graham crackers
1 tablespoon sugar
1 tablespoon cornstarch
⅛ teaspoon salt
2 tablespoons unsalted butter, melted
1 large egg white
Baking spray with flour
3 cups 2% reduced-fat milk
⅔ cup sugar, divided
1 tablespoon finely chopped peeled fresh ginger

1 tablespoon cardamom pods, lightly crushed
1 teaspoon whole cloves
⅛ teaspoon salt
2 (3-inch) cinnamon sticks, broken
2 black tea bags
¼ cup cornstarch
2 large eggs
2 tablespoons unsalted butter
1 cup frozen fat-free whipped topping, thawed
¼ teaspoon ground cinnamon

1. Preheat oven to 350°.

2. Place crackers, 1 tablespoon sugar, 1 tablespoon cornstarch, and salt in a food processor; process until finely ground. Add melted butter and egg white; pulse 3 to 4 times or until mixture is well combined and moist (do not overprocess). Press mixture into the bottom and up the sides of a 9-inch pie plate lightly coated with baking spray. Bake at 350° for 12 minutes or until browned. Cool completely on a wire rack.

3. Combine milk, ⅓ cup sugar, and next 5 ingredients (through cinnamon sticks) in a saucepan. Bring to a boil. Remove pan from heat; add tea bags. Cover and let stand 20 minutes, stirring occasionally.

4. Pour milk mixture through a sieve over a bowl, pressing on tea bags; discard solids. Return milk mixture to pan; bring to a simmer. Combine ⅓ cup sugar, ¼ cup cornstarch, and eggs in a bowl; stir well with a whisk. Gradually add hot milk to egg mixture, stirring constantly with a whisk. Return mixture to pan; cook over medium heat until thick and bubbly, about 5 minutes, stirring constantly. Remove from heat; add butter, stirring until butter melts.

5. Place pan in a large ice-filled bowl for 10 minutes or until room temperature, stirring occasionally. Spoon filling into prepared crust; cover surface with plastic wrap. Chill 3 hours or until set. To serve, top slices with whipped topping, and sprinkle with ground cinnamon.

SERVES 8 (serving size: 1 slice and 2 tablespoons whipped topping)
CALORIES 290; FAT 9.6g (sat 5.2g, mono 2.5g, poly 0.5g); PROTEIN 6g;
CARB 45g; FIBER 1g; CHOL 69mg; IRON 1mg; SODIUM 242mg; CALC 204mg

TECHNIQUE TIP

Traditionally, chai is Indian black tea steeped with a mix of spices, such as cardamom, cinnamon, and black pepper. I like a spice-rich mix, so I added fresh ginger and whole cloves to the filling. Using fresh whole spices is the secret to great chai because they are robust with flavor, natural oils, and aromas. Ground spices lose their potency pretty quickly—six months or so—and become dusty tasting if left on the shelf too long.

MEXICAN CHOCOLATE CREAM PIE

Hands-on: 35 min. Total: 4 hr.

Cinnamon and coffee are common ingredients in Mexican-style chocolate, but adding ground red pepper gives this pie a nice kick.

1½ cups graham cracker crumbs
½ cup plus 2 tablespoons sugar, divided
3 tablespoons cornstarch, divided
1 teaspoon ground cinnamon
⅛ teaspoon salt
2 tablespoons unsalted butter, melted
1 large egg, separated
Baking spray with flour

1 tablespoon unsweetened cocoa
¼ teaspoon instant espresso or instant coffee (optional)
⅛ teaspoon ground red pepper
1 large egg
1¾ cups whole milk
2 ounces bittersweet chocolate, finely chopped
1½ cups frozen fat-free whipped topping, thawed

1. Preheat oven to 350°.

2. Reserve 1 tablespoon crumbs for topping. Combine remaining crumbs, 2 tablespoons sugar, 1 tablespoon cornstarch, cinnamon, and salt in a bowl, stirring well. Add butter and 2 tablespoons of the egg white (reserve the yolk for the filling); toss with a fork until mixture is moist but still crumbly. Press crumb mixture into a 9-inch pie plate coated with baking spray. Bake at 350° for 9 minutes or until lightly toasted; cool completely on a wire rack.

3. Combine reserved egg yolk, ½ cup sugar, 2 tablespoons cornstarch, 1 tablespoon cocoa, espresso, if desired, pepper, and egg in a bowl, stirring well with a whisk. Place milk in a medium saucepan over medium heat; cook until milk reaches 180° or until tiny bubbles form around edge. Gradually add hot milk to egg mixture, stirring constantly with a whisk. Return milk mixture to pan; cook over medium heat 10 minutes or until thick and bubbly, stirring constantly. Remove from heat. Add chocolate; stir until smooth.

4. Place pan in a large ice-filled bowl for 10 minutes or until mixture cools, stirring occasionally. Spoon filling into crust, and cover surface of filling with plastic wrap. Chill 3 hours or until set; remove plastic wrap. Spread whipped topping over pie; sprinkle with reserved cracker crumbs.

SERVES 8 (serving size: 1 slice)
CALORIES 291; FAT 11.1g (sat 5.1g, mono 2.6g, poly 1.3g); PROTEIN 5g;
CARB 44g; FIBER 1g; CHOL 59mg; IRON 1mg; SODIUM 175mg; CALC 77mg

MY TOP 5 TIPS FOR
MAKING LIGHT PIECRUSTS
IN A FOOD PROCESSOR

*Making piecrust with a food processor is the ultimate
way to get flaky crust when using smaller amounts
of fat and minimal amounts of added water.*

1 One thing to keep an eye on when making pie dough in a food processor is overprocessing, which can lead to disappointing results. The trick is knowing how long one pulse is and keeping the number of pulses to a minimum. A food processor pulse is 1 second (think about the length of time it takes to say "1 Mississippi")—no longer, no shorter.

2 When adding fat to the flour mixture, start by cutting it into about 1/2-inch cubes. Scatter the cubes over the top of the flour, and then pulse the recommended number of times indicated in the recipe.

3 When making pie dough, it's best to leave the butter in larger bits, about the size of dried peas. Keeping the butter in larger pieces will create pockets of steam as the butter melts in the oven, which will in turn create lovely flaky layers of pastry.

4 If making rich pie dough (like on page 77), pulse the fat into the flour until the mixture looks like coarse sand. Pulsing the butter into tiny pieces coats more of the flour with the fat, which makes a more tender crust—kind of like the texture of a sugar cookie.

5 When the liquid is added to the food processor, sprinkle it evenly over the entire surface of the flour mixture so that there isn't an overly wet area. This will also help prevent the dough from becoming gummy and clumping together.

HONEY-PECAN TART
WITH CHOCOLATE DRIZZLE

Hands-on: 29 min. Total: 1 hr. 34 min.

CRUST:

1 cup pecan halves
5.6 ounces all-purpose flour
(about 1¼ cups)
½ cup powdered sugar
¼ teaspoon salt
3 tablespoons unsalted butter,
chilled and diced
1 large egg
1 large egg, separated
Baking spray with flour

FILLING:

½ cup light-colored corn syrup
⅓ cup packed brown sugar
¼ cup honey
2 tablespoons unsalted butter,
melted
½ teaspoon vanilla extract
⅛ teaspoon salt
2 large eggs, lightly beaten
1 large egg white, lightly beaten
1 ounce bittersweet chocolate,
finely chopped

1. Preheat oven to 350°.

2. Arrange pecans in a single layer on a baking sheet. Bake at 350° for 8 minutes or until lightly toasted, stirring after 4 minutes. Cool completely.

3. To prepare crust, weigh or lightly spoon flour into dry measuring cups; level with a knife. Place flour, ¼ cup toasted pecans, powdered sugar, and salt in a food processor; process until finely ground. Add butter; pulse 3 to 4 times or until mixture looks sandy. Add egg and egg yolk (reserving the white for the filling); pulse 3 to 4 times or until just combined. Scrape mixture onto a lightly floured work surface; press mixture together to form a disc. Cover with plastic wrap; chill 30 minutes.

4. Unwrap dough, and place on a lightly floured work surface. Roll into an 11-inch circle. Gently fit dough into a 9-inch round removable-bottom metal tart pan lightly coated with baking spray. Gently press dough against bottom and sides of pan; trim edges. Line bottom of dough with parchment paper; arrange pie weights or dried beans on parchment paper. Bake at 350° for 15 minutes or until edges are beginning to brown. Remove pie weights and parchment paper.

5. To prepare filling, combine reserved egg white, corn syrup, and next 7 ingredients in a bowl, stirring until well combined. Stir in ¾ cup toasted pecans. Pour pecan mixture into prepared crust. Bake at 350° for 25 minutes or until just set. Cool completely in pan on a wire rack. Remove sides of tart pan; slide tart onto a serving plate.

6. Place chocolate in a microwave-safe bowl. Microwave at HIGH 1 minute or until chocolate melts, stirring every 15 seconds. Drizzle chocolate over top of tart.

SERVES 12 (serving size: 1 wedge)

CALORIES 291; FAT 13.6g (sat 4.7g, mono 5.3g, poly 2.4g); PROTEIN 4g;
CARB 41g; FIBER 1g; CHOL 75mg; IRON 1mg; SODIUM 108mg; CALC 26mg

HONEY

If you prefer a bold honey flavor, use buckwheat or eucalyptus honey; for mild honey flavor use wildflower or clover. Honey has a more concentrated sugar content than granulated sugar or corn syrup. A higher amount of sugar draws in more moisture from its surroundings, keeping baked goods from drying out for a longer time.

BLUEBERRY-RICOTTA-TEFF TART

Hands-on: 25 min. Total: 2 hr. 15 min.

Lighter than cheesecake but with the same satisfying creamy texture, ricotta fillings offer the perfect canvas to showcase peak-season fruit. Use any berry that is at its ultimate best.

2.25 ounces all-purpose flour (about ½ cup)
3 ounces teff flour (about ½ cup)
¼ teaspoon salt
3 tablespoons granulated sugar
1 tablespoon canola oil
1 large egg
Baking spray with flour
2 cups part-skim ricotta cheese
2 ounces ⅓-less-fat cream cheese, softened
2 teaspoons grated lemon rind, divided
2 tablespoons fresh lemon juice
¼ cup powdered sugar
1 teaspoon vanilla extract
⅛ teaspoon salt
¼ teaspoon baking powder
1 large egg
1 large egg yolk
3 cups fresh blueberries
1½ tablespoons honey

1. Preheat oven to 350°.

2. Weigh or lightly spoon flours into dry measuring cups; level with a knife. Combine flours and salt in a bowl, stirring with a whisk. Place granulated sugar, oil, and egg in a large bowl; beat with a mixer at medium speed 2 minutes or until well combined. Add flour mixture; beat until just combined. Roll dough into an 11-inch circle on a lightly floured surface. Fit dough into a 9-inch removable-bottom tart pan lightly coated with baking spray. Press dough against bottom and sides of pan. (Dough is soft and can be patched with good results.) Chill 15 minutes.

3. Line bottom of dough with parchment paper; arrange pie weights or dried beans on parchment paper. Bake at 350° for 15 minutes or until edge is lightly browned. Remove pie weights and parchment paper; bake an additional 5 minutes. Cool completely on a wire rack.

4. Place ricotta and cream cheese in a bowl; beat with a mixer at medium speed 2 minutes or until smooth. Add 1½ teaspoons lemon rind and next 7 ingredients (through egg yolk); beat at low speed 2 minutes or until well combined. Pour filling into prepared crust. Bake at 350° for 25 minutes or until just set. Cool completely in pan on a wire rack. Remove tart from pan.

5. Combine berries and honey, tossing gently to coat. Arrange berry mixture on top of tart. Sprinkle top with ½ teaspoon rind.

SERVES 8 (serving size: 1 wedge)
CALORIES 292; FAT 10.7g (sat 4.7g, mono 3.7g, poly 1.2g); PROTEIN 12g; CARB 37g; FIBER 3g; CHOL 94mg; IRON 2mg; SODIUM 231mg; CALC 219mg

TEFF

Teff is a tiny, gluten-free grain—about the size of a poppy seed—that has a nutty, earthy flavor. Teff flour is finely ground and an easy way to incorporate whole grains into your baked goods. It is also an excellent source of protein, fiber, and iron and is naturally gluten free. If you'd like to experiment with using teff flour in your baked goods, I would suggest substituting about 25% of the wheat flour with teff flour. I've used a ratio of 50% in this tart to allow the flavor of teff to really shine through.

HAZELNUT, PEAR, AND BLUE CHEESE TART

Hands-on: 17 min. Total: 2 hr. 3 min.

¾ cup toasted hazelnuts, divided
5 tablespoons sugar, divided
2 tablespoons unsalted butter, softened
½ teaspoon salt, divided
1 large egg
4.5 ounces all-purpose flour (about 1 cup)
Baking spray with flour

2 large ripe Bartlett pears, peeled, cored, and cut lengthwise into ⅛-inch-thick slices
2 tablespoons unsalted butter, melted
1 tablespoon cornstarch
1 tablespoon fresh lemon juice
2 tablespoons apple jelly
2 tablespoons crumbled blue cheese

1. Place ¼ cup hazelnuts in a small bowl; set aside. Place ½ cup hazelnuts and 3 tablespoons sugar in a food processor; process until finely ground. Combine hazelnut mixture, softened butter, ¼ teaspoon salt, and egg in a bowl; beat with a mixer at medium speed until well combined. Weigh or lightly spoon flour into a dry measuring cup; level with a knife. Add flour; beat at low speed until just combined. Press mixture into a 4-inch disc on plastic wrap; cover. Chill 1 hour.

2. Preheat oven to 350°. Place oven rack in lower third of oven.

3. Unwrap dough; place on a lightly floured work surface. Roll into an 11-inch circle. Place dough into a 9-inch removable-bottom tart pan lightly coated with baking spray. Press dough against bottom and sides of pan. (Dough is very soft and may be patched with good results.) Line bottom of dough with parchment paper; arrange pie weights or dried beans on parchment paper. Bake in lower third of oven at 350° for 11 minutes or until edge is just beginning to brown. Remove pie weights and parchment paper; bake 5 minutes. Cool completely on a wire rack.

4. Gently toss pear slices with 2 tablespoons sugar, melted butter, cornstarch, juice, and ¼ teaspoon salt. Arrange pear slices spoke-like in crust. Bake at 350° for 30 minutes or until pears are tender when pierced with the tip of a knife. Remove tart from oven.

5. Place jelly in a microwave-safe bowl; microwave at HIGH 30 seconds or until jelly boils. Brush top of tart with jelly. Cool completely in pan on a wire rack. Remove from pan. Coarsely chop reserved ¼ cup hazelnuts. Sprinkle tart with nuts and blue cheese.

SERVES 8 (serving size: 1 wedge)
CALORIES 284; FAT 14.9g (sat 4.8g, mono 7.7g, poly 1.4g); PROTEIN 5g;
CARB 35g; FIBER 3g; CHOL 40mg; IRON 2mg; SODIUM 186mg; CALC 39mg

MAKING THE CRUST

1. Fold the edge of the dough towards the inside and press it into the sides of the tart pan, making a thicker edge.

2. Crumpling the parchment paper before fitting it into the tart makes it easier to handle and fit against the dough. Make sure there are enough pie weights to completely cover the bottom and slightly come up the sides of the pan.

3. Pre-baking the dough (also referred to as blind baking) in the lower third of the oven helps create a crisper bottom crust, especially useful if the filling has juicy fruit.

CHERRY-ALMOND MINI CROSTATAS

Hands-on: 40 min. Total: 2 hr. 24 min.

The Italian crostata is very similar to the French galette; both are rustic fruit tarts, simple and rich with seasonal fruit. This version is baked in a tart pan because I wanted to enrich the crust with egg, sugar, and almond flour, which makes the crust softer and more difficult to pleat around the fruit like a free-form galette. When working with delicate, butter-rich dough, keep it as cold as possible but still pliable.

¼ cup almond flour
4.5 ounces all-purpose flour (about 1 cup)
½ teaspoon salt, divided
¼ cup unsalted butter, softened
¾ cup granulated sugar, divided
1 large egg
Baking spray with flour

1½ pounds fresh cherries, pitted and halved
2 tablespoons cornstarch
1 tablespoon fresh lemon juice
1 tablespoon unsalted butter, melted
3 tablespoons sliced almonds
1 tablespoon powdered sugar

1. Preheat oven to 375°. Place oven rack in lower third of oven.

2. Sprinkle almond flour on a baking sheet. Bake at 375° for 6 minutes or until beginning to brown, stirring after 3 minutes. Cool completely on pan.

3. Weigh or lightly spoon all-purpose flour into a dry measuring cup; level with a knife. Combine flours and ¼ teaspoon salt in a bowl. Place softened butter and ¼ cup granulated sugar in a large bowl; beat at medium speed 1 minute or until well combined. Add egg; beat 1 minute or until well combined. Add flour mixture; beat at low speed until just combined. Shape into a ball. Press mixture into a 4-inch disc on plastic wrap; cover. Chill 30 minutes.

4. Unwrap dough, and place on a lightly floured work surface. Divide the dough in 8 equal portions, and press into 4-inch mini tart shells lightly coated with baking spray. Press dough against bottom and sides of tart shells.

5. Combine cherries, ¼ teaspoon salt, ½ cup granulated sugar, cornstarch, juice, and melted butter in a bowl; toss gently to combine. Divide mixture among prepared crusts. Sprinkle nuts on top. Bake at 375° in lower third of oven for 25 to 30 minutes or until golden brown and bubbly. Shield edges of tarts with foil if getting too brown. Cool completely in pans on a wire rack. Remove crostatas from pans. Sift powdered sugar over top of each.

SERVES 8 (serving size: 1 crostata)
CALORIES 300; FAT 11g (sat 5g, mono 2.8g, poly 0.8g); PROTEIN 5g;
CARB 49g; FIBER 3g; CHOL 42mg; IRON 1mg; SODIUM 157mg; CALC 33mg

TECHNIQUE TIP

To make a full-size tart, roll the dough into an 11-inch circle, and then press into a 9-inch removable-bottom tart pan. Bake at 375° for 45 minutes. If your cherries are super juicy, add an extra tablespoon of cornstarch with the cherries to help soak up their luscious juice. And the opposite applies too; if the cherries seem a little dry, decrease the total cornstarch to 1 tablespoon.

CINNAMON-APPLE UPSIDE-DOWN TART

Hands-on: 35 min. Total: 1 hr. 45 min.

This is kind of like the classic French Tarte Tatin, but lighter, quicker, and easier to make. Use a combination of apples for deeper apple flavor and texture. If you don't have a cast-iron skillet, you can use any 10-inch ovenproof skillet. And, if it seems too risky to flip the finished tart onto a serving plate, simply scoop it right from the pan.

CRUST:
5.6 ounces all-purpose flour
　(about 1¼ cups)
¼ teaspoon baking powder
¼ teaspoon salt
2 tablespoons unsalted butter,
　cold
2 tablespoons natural shortening
　(such as Earth Balance), chilled
3 tablespoons ice water
1 teaspoon white vinegar

FILLING:
6 cups peeled 1-inch pieces apple
　(such as Honey Crisp, Golden
　Delicious, and Granny Smith)
½ cup unsweetened apple juice

½ cup packed brown sugar
2 tablespoons unsalted butter,
　melted
1½ teaspoons ground cinnamon
⅛ teaspoon salt
Cooking spray
2 tablespoons cornstarch
2 tablespoons water

TOPPING:
1.5 ounces ⅓-less-fat cream
　cheese, softened
2 tablespoons heavy whipping
　cream
2 tablespoons powdered sugar
¼ teaspoon vanilla extract

1. To prepare crust, weigh or lightly spoon flour into dry measuring cups; level with a knife. Place flour, baking powder, and salt in a food processor; process to combine. Cut butter and shortening into ½-inch pieces; add to processor. Pulse 2 to 3 times or until butter is about the size of dried peas. Sprinkle ice water and vinegar over mixture. Pulse 2 to 3 times or until mixture is combined and looks like coarse sand. (Do not overprocess mixture; it will become clumpy and tough.)

2. Scrape mixture onto a lightly floured work surface. Gather mixture together, and press into a 4-inch disc. Cover disc with plastic wrap, and chill 30 minutes. (The dough can be made 1 day ahead; if chilled 24 hours, let stand at room temperature 10 minutes before rolling).

3. Preheat oven to 400°.

4. To prepare filling, place apples and next 5 ingredients (through salt) in a large bowl; toss well to combine. Pour apple mixture into a 10-inch cast-iron skillet coated with cooking spray; bring to a boil. Cook on medium-high heat 10 minutes or until apples begin to soften. Combine cornstarch and 2 tablespoons water in a small bowl, stirring until smooth. Slowly pour cornstarch mixture into apple mixture, stirring constantly. Cook 1 minute or until mixture thickens, stirring constantly. Remove pan from heat; let stand 5 minutes. Stir apple mixture to loosen browned bits.

5. Unwrap dough, and place on a lightly floured work surface. Roll into an 11-inch circle. Place over apple mixture, tucking dough down between apples and skillet. Bake at 400° for 37 minutes or until well browned and bubbly around edge. Cool in pan 15 minutes on a wire rack. Carefully invert tart onto a plate.

6. To prepare topping, beat cream cheese and remaining ingredients at medium speed 2 minutes or until smooth and fluffy. Dollop topping onto servings.

SERVES 10 (serving size: 1 wedge and about 1 tablespoon topping)
CALORIES 247; FAT 10g (sat 5.2g, mono 2.9g, poly 1g); PROTEIN 2g; CARB 38g;
FIBER 2g; CHOL 19mg; IRON 1mg; SODIUM 120mg; CALC 36mg

BLACKBERRY-PEAR GALETTE

Hands-on: 30 min. Total: 1 hr. 30 min.

Khorasan wheat—sold under the brand name Kamut—is loaded with nutritional goodness and has a wonderful nutty, buttery flavor. If you can't find it at your specialty grocery store, substitute whole-wheat pastry flour to keep whole grains in the pastry crust. It's best to assemble the filling after you roll out the pastry so it doesn't start to juice out too soon—you want all those lovely juices inside the galette.

SHAPING A GALETTE

PASTRY:

4.5 ounces all-purpose flour (about 1 cup)
4 ounces Kamut flour (about ⅔ cup)
¼ teaspoon salt
¼ cup granulated sugar
3 tablespoons unsalted butter
1 large egg
1 large egg, separated and divided

FILLING:

3 cups fresh blackberries
2 large ripe pears, peeled and chopped
¼ cup granulated sugar
2 tablespoons cornstarch
2 tablespoons unsalted butter, melted
1 tablespoon fresh lemon juice
½ teaspoon freshly ground nutmeg
⅛ teaspoon salt
1 tablespoon turbinado sugar

1. Preheat oven to 350°.

2. To prepare pastry, weigh or lightly spoon flours into dry measuring cups; level with a knife. Combine flours and salt in a bowl, stirring with a whisk. Place granulated sugar and butter in a bowl; beat with a mixer at medium speed until light and fluffy. Add egg and egg yolk; beat until well combined. Add flour mixture; beat at low speed until mixture holds together. Roll dough to a 14-inch circle on lightly floured parchment paper; place on a baking sheet.

3. To prepare filling, combine blackberries and next 7 ingredients in a bowl; gently toss to combine. Mound blackberry mixture in center of dough, leaving a 2-inch border. Fold edges of dough over berry mixture, pressing gently to seal (dough will only partially cover berry mixture).

4. Beat reserved egg white in a small bowl. Brush dough with egg white, and sprinkle with turbinado sugar. Bake at 350° for 50 minutes or until golden brown and bubbly. Let stand 10 minutes before serving.

SERVES 8 (serving size: 1 wedge)
CALORIES 283; FAT 9.1g (sat 5g, mono 2.4g, poly 0.7g); PROTEIN 5g;
CARB 47g; FIBER 6g; CHOL 66mg; IRON 2mg; SODIUM 129mg; CALC 32mg

1. Use lightly floured parchment paper when you roll the dough out so you will be able to pop the whole thing in the oven when assembled. Flouring the paper makes it easier to fold up the edges for encasing the juicy filling.

2. After mounding the filling in the center of the dough, fold about a 3-inch section of the dough up onto the filling.

3. Continue folding 3-inch sections up over the filling, pressing the dough together at the pleated sections. Brushing the dough with lightly beaten egg white and sprinkling with sugar helps the dough become golden brown and crisp.

APRICOT-PISTACHIO TART
WITH WHIPPED GOAT CHEESE

Hands-on: 25 min. Total: 2 hr. 20 min.

½ cup lightly salted roasted pistachios, divided

5 tablespoons granulated sugar, divided

4.5 ounces all-purpose flour (about 1 cup)

½ teaspoon salt, divided

3 tablespoons unsalted butter, softened

1 large egg

Baking spray with flour

2 pounds ripe apricots, quartered

3 tablespoons apricot jam

2 tablespoons cornstarch

3 tablespoons heavy whipping cream

3 tablespoons powdered sugar

1 ounce goat cheese

2 teaspoons honey

1. Set aside 3 tablespoons pistachios. Place remaining pistachios and 2 tablespoons sugar in a food processor; process until finely ground. Weigh or lightly spoon flour into a dry measuring cup; level with a knife. Add flour and ¼ teaspoon salt to processor; pulse to combine. Place 3 tablespoons sugar and butter in a large bowl; beat with a mixer at medium speed 2 minutes or until well combined. Add egg; beat until combined. Add flour mixture; beat at low speed until just combined. Press mixture into a 4-inch circle; wrap in plastic wrap. Chill 30 minutes.

2. Preheat oven to 350°.

3. Unwrap dough; place on a lightly floured work surface. Roll into an 11-inch circle or square. Fit dough into a 9-inch removable-bottom tart pan lightly coated with baking spray. Press dough against bottom and sides of pan. (Pastry is very soft and can be patched with good results.) Line bottom of dough with parchment paper lightly coated with baking spray; arrange pie weights or dried beans on parchment paper. Bake at 350° for 15 minutes or until edges begin to brown. Remove from oven; remove parchment paper and pie weights. Cool slightly (10 minutes).

4. Combine apricots, jam, cornstarch, and ¼ teaspoon salt in a bowl; toss gently. Arrange apricot mixture in prepared crust. Bake at 350° for 1 hour or until golden brown and bubbly. Shield edges with foil if getting too brown. Cool completely in pan on wire rack. Remove from pan.

5. Combine cream, powdered sugar, cheese, and honey in a bowl; beat at medium speed until light and fluffy. Chop reserved 3 tablespoons pistachios. To serve, top each wedge with about 2 teaspoons topping, and sprinkle with about ½ tablespoon pistachios.

SERVES 8 (serving size: 1 wedge)

CALORIES 299; FAT 12.1g (sat 5.4g, mono 4.1g, poly 1.5g); PROTEIN 6g; CARB 45g; FIBER 3g; CHOL 45mg; IRON 2mg; SODIUM 182mg; CALC 47mg

APRICOTS

Apricot season is short, so don't let it slip by without making this tart. Choose ripe apricots—those that give a little when pressed and are a rich coral color. The pits are easy to remove: Just run a knife around the apricot, starting at the stem end, open it up, and pluck out the pit.

SMALL BITES

SPICED APPLE TWO-BITE TARTS

Hands-on: 40 min. Total: 60 min.

⅓ cup sugar
4 tablespoons unsalted butter, softened
2 tablespoons canola oil
1 tablespoon 1% low-fat milk
½ teaspoon vanilla extract
¼ teaspoon salt
4.5 ounces all-purpose flour (about 1 cup)
⅓ cup very finely chopped toasted pecans
Baking spray with flour
2 cups finely diced apple (such as Golden Delicious or Honey Crisp)

2 teaspoons fresh lemon juice
2 tablespoons sugar
½ teaspoon ground cinnamon
¼ teaspoon salt
¼ teaspoon ground allspice
⅛ teaspoon ground ginger
1 tablespoon unsalted butter
½ teaspoon cornstarch
1 tablespoon water
¼ cup crème fraîche
24 tiny mint leaves (optional)

1. Preheat oven to 350°.

2. Place first 6 ingredients in a medium bowl. Beat with a mixer at medium speed 1 minute or until well combined. Weigh or lightly spoon flour into a dry measuring cup; level with a knife. Add flour to butter mixture; beat until just combined. Add nuts; beat until just combined. Divide dough evenly into 24 pieces; shape into balls. Place dough balls into 24 miniature muffin cups coated with baking spray. Press dough into bottom and up sides of muffin cups, forming a bowl. Bake at 350° for 10 to 11 minutes or until golden brown. Cool in pan on a wire rack 5 minutes. Carefully remove from pan; cool completely on wire rack.

3. Place diced apple and lemon juice in a bowl; toss to coat. Add sugar and next 4 ingredients (through ginger); toss well.

4. Melt butter in a medium saucepan over medium heat. Add apple mixture. Cover and cook 10 minutes or until apple is tender, stirring occasionally. Combine cornstarch and 1 tablespoon water in a small bowl. Stir cornstarch mixture into apple mixture; cook 1 minute or until mixture thickens, stirring constantly. Place apple mixture into a bowl; cool to room temperature. Spoon about 2 teaspoons apple mixture into each tart shell. Top with about 1 teaspoon crème fraîche. Arrange a mint leaf on top, if desired.

SERVES 12 (serving size: 2 tarts)
CALORIES 184; FAT 11.3g (sat 4.6g, mono 4g, poly 1.6g); PROTEIN 2g;
CARB 20g; FIBER 1g; CHOL 19mg; IRON 1mg; SODIUM 100mg; CALC 13mg

TECHNIQUE TIP

These sweet little tarts can be made ahead. The nutty shells can be prepared two to three days in advance. Just keep them in an airtight container until you are ready to fill them. The apple filling can be made and stored covered in the refrigerator for up to two days. Just bring the filling back to room temperature before scooping into the shells to get the full apple flavor.

PECAN MINI TARTS

Hands-on: 55 min. Total: 1 hr. 10 min.

These baby bites rich with eggs, brown sugar, and half-and-half will satisfy every sweet tooth. The glaze is extra thick so that it stands up on the tarts instead of melting into the filling.

FILLING:
⅓ cup packed brown sugar
⅓ cup half-and-half
¼ cup dark corn syrup
1 tablespoon cornstarch
Dash of salt
2 large egg yolks
2 tablespoons unsalted butter
¼ teaspoon vanilla extract
⅔ cup chopped toasted pecans

TART SHELLS:
⅓ cup granulated sugar
4 tablespoons unsalted butter,
   softened

2 tablespoons canola oil
1 tablespoon half-and-half
½ teaspoon vanilla extract
¼ teaspoon salt
4.5 ounces all-purpose flour
   (about 1 cup)
⅓ cup toasted pecans, finely
   chopped
Baking spray with flour

GLAZE STRIPE:
⅔ cup powdered sugar
1½ teaspoons half-and-half
¼ teaspoon vanilla extract
Dash of salt

1. Preheat oven to 350°.

2. To prepare filling, place first 6 ingredients in a small saucepan over medium heat; bring to a boil, stirring constantly. Cook 30 seconds, stirring constantly. Remove pan from heat. Add 2 tablespoons butter and ¼ teaspoon vanilla, stirring until butter melts. Stir in ⅔ cup pecans. Scoop mixture into a bowl; cover and chill 30 minutes.

3. To prepare tart shells, place ⅓ cup sugar and next 5 ingredients (through salt) in a medium bowl. Beat with a mixer at medium speed 1 minute or until well combined. Weigh or lightly spoon flour into a dry measuring cup; level with a knife. Add flour to butter mixture; beat until just combined. Add nuts; beat until just combined. Divide dough evenly into 24 pieces; shape into balls. Place dough balls into 24 miniature muffin cups coated with baking spray. Press dough into bottom and up sides of muffin cups, forming a bowl. Bake at 350° for 10 to 11 minutes or until golden brown. Cool in pan on a wire rack 5 minutes. Carefully remove from pan; cool completely on wire rack. Spoon about 1 tablespoon filling into each tart shell.

4. To prepare glaze, combine powdered sugar, half-and-half, vanilla, and salt in a small bowl; stir with a whisk until smooth. Spoon glaze into a small zip-top plastic bag. Snip a tiny hole in bottom corner of bag; stripe tarts with glaze.

SERVES 12 (serving size: 2 tarts)

CALORIES 287; FAT 16.5g (sat 5.3g, mono 7.3g, poly 3g); PROTEIN 3g; CARB 34g; FIBER 1g; CHOL 49mg; IRON 1mg; SODIUM 91mg; CALC 29mg

CANDY APPLE MINI MUFFINS

Hands-on: 14 min. Total: 24 min.

Remember crunchy cinnamon candy-coated apples at the county fair? These mini muffins are a great way to keep those memories alive—and they're ready in less than 25 minutes!

1 Granny Smith or other tart apple, grated (1 cup)
⅔ cup granulated sugar, divided
6 tablespoons unsalted butter, melted
1 teaspoon vanilla extract
2 large eggs
6.75 ounces all-purpose flour (about 1½ cups)
½ teaspoon baking powder
½ teaspoon salt
½ teaspoon ground cinnamon
¼ teaspoon baking soda
2 ounces cinnamon decorator candies (such as Red Hots)
Baking spray with flour
1 tablespoon powdered sugar

1. Preheat oven to 350°.

2. Place apple and ⅓ cup sugar in a bowl; toss well to combine.

3. Combine ⅓ cup sugar, butter, vanilla, and eggs in a medium bowl, stirring with a whisk.

4. Weigh or lightly spoon flour into dry measuring cups; level with a knife. Combine flour, baking powder, salt, cinnamon, and baking soda in a large bowl; stir with a whisk. Add apple mixture, butter mixture, and cinnamon candy; stir just until combined. Scoop batter evenly into 24 miniature muffin cups coated with baking spray. Bake at 350° for 8 to 10 minutes or until a wooden pick inserted in center comes out clean. Remove muffins from pan; cool on a wire rack. Sift powdered sugar over tops of muffins.

SERVES 12 (serving size: 2 muffins)
CALORIES 195; FAT 6.7g (sat 3.9g, mono 1.8g, poly 0.4g); PROTEIN 3g; CARB 31g; FIBER 1g; CHOL 46mg; IRON 1mg; SODIUM 157mg; CALC 22mg

TECHNIQUE TIP

Tossing the grated apple with part of the sugar breaks down the apple's fibers and speeds up the baking time. Using a tart apple like Granny Smith gives a great apple flavor to the muffins, but Honey Crisp, Golden Delicious, or Braeburn would be wonderful, too.

STAMPED LEMON SUGAR COOKIES

Hands-on: 27 min. Total: 2 hr. 12 min.

1. Coating the cookies in sugar gives them a nice sweet crunch on the outside and helps them to not dry out too quickly.

2. If you don't have cookie stamps, use the bottom of a glass, the ridged side of a meat tenderizer, a fork, your fingers, or really anything to press the cookies into a disc.

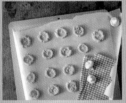

3. Letting the cookies stand for 1 hour after imprinting with the stamp or other tool is a trick borrowed from the German springerle cookie. Allowing them to dry out a little on the outside helps retain the stamp's imprint during baking.

When my daughter, Barbra, was in first grade, she made me the sweetest cookie stamps out of fired clay for Mother's Day. The teacher (Mrs. Kemp) sent along a recipe for shortbread cookies that were delicious. Shortbread cookies traditionally have a lot of butter—too much to qualify as light. This version is nice and tender with a short texture and makes a sweet stamped cookie (see the technique for some stamping ideas). Barbra is now a teacher and an education coordinator for first through eighth grade homeschoolers in California, and she loves helping her students create treasured homemade gifts for their mothers.

4.5 ounces all-purpose flour (about 1 cup)
¼ teaspoon salt
¼ teaspoon baking powder
⅔ cup plus 2 tablespoons sugar, divided

¼ cup unsalted butter
2 tablespoons canola oil
1 tablespoon grated lemon rind
½ teaspoon vanilla extract
1 large egg yolk

1. Weigh or lightly spoon flour into a dry measuring cup; level with a knife. Combine flour, salt, and baking powder in a bowl; stir with a whisk.

2. Place ⅔ cup sugar and remaining ingredients in a large bowl; beat with a mixer at medium speed 5 minutes or until well combined. Add flour mixture; beat at low speed until just combined (about 30 seconds). Wrap in plastic wrap; chill 30 minutes.

3. Place 2 tablespoons sugar in a shallow dish. Shape dough into 18 balls; roll balls in sugar. Place balls 3 inches apart on baking sheets covered with parchment paper. Press cookies gently with a cookie stamp or another textured tool. Let stand at room temperature 1 hour.

4. Preheat oven to 325°.

5. Bake at 325° for 13 minutes or until just beginning to brown on edges. Cool on pan 2 minutes. Cool completely on wire racks.

SERVES 18 (serving size: 1 cookie)
CALORIES 100; FAT 4.4g (sat 1.8g, mono 1.8g, poly 0.6g); PROTEIN 1g; CARB 14g; FIBER 0g; CHOL 17mg; IRON 0mg; SODIUM 40mg; CALC 7mg

MY TOP 5 TIPS FOR
MAKING COOKIES

The fragrance of baking cookies can conjure strong memories more quickly in my mind than anything else. I fondly remember Christmases past, crazy fun Halloween parties, and gifts for new mothers and ailing neighbors. Use these tips to lovingly make some memories of your own.

1 *I love the Zen of cookie baking. A lot of people don't like to make cookies because they feel it is too repetitive and boring. For me, it's about how I can make the final cookie look just as pretty as the first, or maybe even better. I use a small ice-cream scoop to make the size consistent from beginning to end.*

2 *Watch the bake time closely. The goal is to create cookies with crispy edges and a soft, chewy center. When in doubt, underbaking the cookies by a minute or so is far better than overbaking and ending up with a dry, crumbly, semiburned cookie.*

3 *Don't overprocess cookie dough. When adding the flour mixture to the mixing bowl, beat on low speed just until the flour gets mixed in. Or even better, pull the dough off the mixer before all the flour is mixed in and finish mixing it by hand. Gentle mixing leads to more tender cookies.*

4 *Don't skimp on the time the cookie dough chills in the refrigerator. Chilling the dough will help the cookies retain their shape and not spread all over the baking sheet. When the cookie dough is cold, the oven's heat sets the outsides before the insides are done and helps with crispy edges and chewy centers.*

5 *Baking sheet tips: Don't place cookie dough on a warm or hot baking sheet. If you're baking multiple batches of cookies, cool the baking sheet completely before loading it up with the next batch for the oven. (You can run it under cold water to speed the process. Just be sure to dry it thoroughly.) A warm or hot baking sheet will cause the cookie dough to start spreading and result in an oversized flat greasy cookie with overbaked edges. For fragile cookies or those that you don't want to brown too much, add a second baking sheet to insulate them from the oven's heat. You can double-up right at the start or add a second baking sheet halfway through the bake time to keep those bottoms from overbrowning. This works well on the mini muffin pans, too.*

STAR ANISE SNICKERDOODLES

Hands-on: 30 min. Total: 1 hr. 45 min.

The flavor of star anise is a wonderful mix of fennel, tarragon, and licorice. While not nearly as strong as a black jelly bean (my favorite), it's a great spice to become familiar with in baking and savory applications. Star anise is included in Chinese five-spice and Indian garam masala blends.

5.6 ounces all-purpose flour
  (about 1¼ cups)
1 teaspoon baking powder
1 teaspoon ground star anise
¼ teaspoon salt
¼ teaspoon cream of tartar
6 tablespoons unsalted butter,
  at room temperature
1 cup plus 3 tablespoons sugar,
  divided
½ teaspoon vanilla extract
1 large egg
1 teaspoon ground cinnamon

1. Weigh or lightly spoon flour into dry measuring cups; level with a knife. Combine flour and next 4 ingredients (through cream of tartar) in a bowl; stir with a whisk. Place butter in a medium bowl; beat with a mixer at medium speed 30 seconds or until smooth. Add 1 cup sugar and vanilla to butter; beat 2 minutes or until light and fluffy. Add egg; beat 1 minute or until well combined. Add flour mixture; beat 1 minute at low speed or until just combined. Shape dough into a disc; wrap in plastic wrap. Chill 1 hour.

2. Preheat oven to 375°.

3. Shape dough into 24 balls. Combine 3 tablespoons sugar and cinnamon in a shallow dish. Roll dough balls in cinnamon mixture, coating completely. Place balls 3 inches apart on baking sheets covered with parchment paper. Bake at 375° for 10 minutes or until edges are golden. Cool on pan 5 minutes. Remove from pan, and place on a wire rack to cool.

SERVES 24 (serving size: 1 cookie)
CALORIES 91; FAT 3.1g (sat 1.9g, mono 0.8g, poly 0.2g); PROTEIN 1g; CARB 15g; FIBER 0g; CHOL 15mg; IRON 0mg; SODIUM 48mg; CALC 15mg

STAR ANISE

If you haven't used star anise before, this is a great opportunity to add it to your spice cabinet. Use your electric spice or coffee grinder to pulverize the whole spice into finely ground pieces, and scoop out what you need with a measuring spoon. If you don't have a spice grinder, place the star anise in a heavy zip-top plastic bag, and crush it *very well* with a rolling pin.

MOLASSES COOKIES

Hands-on: 15 min. Total: 60 min.

Sometimes it takes multiple tries to get a recipe right when remaking it into a light recipe. My Aunt Jean makes the best molasses cookies at holiday time, and it took four tries to get this lightened version to be a close second to hers. She makes hers with lots of vegetable shortening (the kind with hydrogenated fat), but this one delivers that same texture using a modest amount of unsalted butter. Aromatic molasses, ginger, cinnamon, and cloves are the stars in this sugar-crusted old-fashioned cookie.

8 ounces all-purpose flour
  (about 1¾ cups)
1 teaspoon ground cinnamon
½ teaspoon baking soda
½ teaspoon ground ginger
½ teaspoon ground cloves
¼ teaspoon baking powder

¼ teaspoon salt
6 tablespoons unsalted butter
8 tablespoons granulated sugar,
  divided
¼ cup packed dark brown sugar
1 large egg
¼ cup molasses

1. Weigh or lightly spoon flour into dry measuring cups; level with a knife. Combine flour and next 6 ingredients (through salt) in a bowl, stirring with a whisk.

2. Place butter, 5 tablespoons granulated sugar, and brown sugar in a large bowl; beat with a mixer at medium speed 5 minutes or until fluffy. Add egg; beat 1 minute or until well combined. Add molasses; beat until just combined. Add flour mixture; beat at low speed 1 minute or until just combined. Cover and chill 30 minutes.

3. Preheat oven to 350°.

4. Shape dough into 24 balls (about 1½ tablespoons each). Place 3 tablespoons sugar in a shallow dish. Roll balls in sugar, covering completely. Place balls 3 inches apart on baking sheets covered with parchment paper. Bake at 350° for 12 minutes or until just set. Cool on pan 3 minutes. Remove from pan, and place on a wire rack to cool.

SERVES 24 (serving size: 1 cookie)
CALORIES 97; FAT 3.2g (sat 1.9g, mono 0.8g, poly 0.2g); PROTEIN 1g;
CARB 16g; FIBER 0g; CHOL 15mg; IRON 1mg; SODIUM 60mg; CALC 15mg

1. Chilling the dough helps it relax and gives it time to hydrate, and a chilled dough won't spread as much in the oven. Using a 2-tablespoon ice-cream scoop evenly and cleanly portions the dough so all the cookies are the same size.

2. The sugar coating is a nice finish to these molasses cookies—it adds a sweet little crunch on the outside and gives them sparkle. Roll the scooped dough into balls with your hands, and then roll them in sugar.

3. Place the sugared dough balls 3 inches apart to give them room to spread. There's no need to flatten them; they'll do that on their own.

CARROT CAKE SANDWICH COOKIES

Hands-on: 30 min. Total: 50 min.

Baking the cookies for only 9 minutes isn't long enough for the carrots to get soft. So to help them get tender, toss the carrots with half of the sugar and let them stand for a few minutes to break down the tough fibers.

2 cups shredded carrots
  (about 2 large)
⅔ cup packed brown sugar,
  divided
4 tablespoons unsalted butter,
  divided
2 tablespoons canola oil
1 teaspoon grated orange rind
  (optional)
¾ teaspoon vanilla extract, divided

1 large egg
4.5 ounces all-purpose flour
  (about 1 cup)
1 teaspoon ground cinnamon
⅜ teaspoon salt, divided
¼ teaspoon baking soda
¼ teaspoon baking powder
4 ounces ⅓-less-fat cream cheese,
  softened
1 cup powdered sugar

1. Preheat oven to 350°.

2. Combine carrots and ⅓ cup brown sugar in a bowl; toss well. Let stand 5 minutes.

3. Place 2 tablespoons butter in a microwave-safe bowl. Microwave at HIGH 30 seconds or until melted. Add oil, rind (if using), ½ teaspoon vanilla, and egg; stir with a whisk until well combined.

4. Weigh or lightly spoon flour into a dry measuring cup; level with a knife. Combine flour, ⅓ cup brown sugar, cinnamon, ¼ teaspoon salt, baking soda, and baking powder in a large bowl; stir well with a whisk. Add carrot mixture and butter mixture; stir until just combined. Drop dough by tablespoonfuls 2 inches apart (you should have 28 cookies) onto baking sheets covered with parchment paper. Bake at 350° for 9 minutes or until set and crisp around the edges. Remove pan from oven; let stand 3 minutes. Remove cookies from pan; cool completely on wire racks.

5. Combine cream cheese, 2 tablespoons butter, ¼ teaspoon vanilla, and ⅛ teaspoon salt in a bowl; beat with a mixer at medium speed 3 minutes or until fluffy. Add powdered sugar; beat at low speed 1 minute or until well combined (do not overbeat). Spread about 1 tablespoon icing on bottom of 1 cookie; top with bottom of second cookie. Repeat procedure with remaining cookies and filling.

SERVES 14 (serving size: 1 cookie sandwich)
CALORIES 186; FAT 7.6g (sat 3.4g, mono 2.7g, poly 0.9g); PROTEIN 2g; CARB 28g; FIBER 1g; CHOL 28mg; IRON 1mg; SODIUM 140mg; CALC 35mg

CHOCOLATE DELUGE COOKIES

Hands-on: 16 min. Total: 1 hr. 15 min.

In culinary school, we made incredible chocolate cookies called Mudslides. This recipe is just as tasty, decadently fudgy, and loaded with chocolate, just a lot lighter in calories.

6.75 ounces all-purpose flour
(about 1½ cups)
6 tablespoons unsweetened
cocoa
½ teaspoon salt
¾ cup sugar
¼ cup unsalted butter, at room
temperature

2 tablespoons canola oil
2 large eggs
¼ teaspoon vanilla extract
½ cup bittersweet chocolate
chips

1. Weigh or lightly spoon flour into dry measuring cups; level with a knife. Combine flour, cocoa, and salt in a bowl, stirring with a whisk.

2. Place sugar, butter, and oil in a bowl; beat at medium speed until well combined, about 5 minutes. Add eggs, 1 at a time, beating well after each addition. Add vanilla; beat 1 minute. Add flour mixture to butter mixture, beating at low speed until just combined. Add chips; beat at low speed until just combined. Cover with plastic wrap, and chill 30 minutes.

3. Preheat oven to 350°.

4. Drop about 2 tablespoons dough 2 inches apart (you should have 24 cookies) on baking sheets covered with parchment paper. Bake at 350° for 8 minutes or until almost set. Cool on pan 2 minutes or until firm. Remove cookies from pan; cool on wire racks.

SERVES 24 (serving size: 1 cookie)
CALORIES 109; FAT 5.2g (sat 2.4g, mono 1.5g, poly 0.5g); PROTEIN 2g;
CARB 15g; FIBER 1g; CHOL 21mg; IRON 1mg; SODIUM 31mg; CALC 6mg

TECHNIQUE TIP

The secret to these rich chocolate cookies is not to overbake them. Leave them a little shiny on top for a creamy cookie center.

CHOPPED CHOCOLATE COOKIES

Hands-on: 21 min. Total: 49 min.

Bittersweet chocolate goes perfectly with the deep flavors of teff flour, oats, and walnuts. If you prefer, coarsely chop the chocolate into bigger pieces.

3.3 ounces all-purpose flour (about ¾ cup)
1.1 ounces teff flour (about ¼ cup)
⅔ cup old-fashioned rolled oats
½ teaspoon baking powder
½ teaspoon baking soda
½ teaspoon salt
½ cup granulated sugar
½ cup packed brown sugar
¼ cup unsalted butter
2 tablespoons canola oil
1 teaspoon vanilla extract
1 large egg
2 ounces bittersweet chocolate, finely chopped
½ cup chopped walnuts

1. Preheat oven to 350°.

2. Weigh or lightly spoon flours into dry measuring cups; level with a knife. Place flours and next 4 ingredients (through salt) in a food processor; process until finely ground.

3. Place sugars, butter, oil, and vanilla in a large bowl; beat with a mixer at medium speed 5 minutes or until light and fluffy. Add egg; beat 1 minute. Add flour mixture; beat at low speed until just combined. Stir in chocolate and nuts. Drop dough by rounded tablespoonfuls (about 1½ tablespoons) 2 inches apart (you should have 24 cookies) onto baking sheets covered with parchment paper. Bake at 350° for 8 minutes or until golden. Let stand on pan until completely cool.

SERVES 24 (serving size: 1 cookie)
CALORIES 115; FAT 5.9g (sat 2g, mono 1.5g, poly 1.6g); PROTEIN 2g; CARB 15g; FIBER 1g; CHOL 12mg; IRON 1mg; SODIUM 86mg; CALC 16mg

HOLIDAY TEA CAKES

Hands-on: 20 min. Total: 2 hr.

This delicate vanilla sponge cookie is a lightened-up madeleine, which is made in a very specific shell-shaped mold. Use any mold you have on hand. The cookie batter can be made ahead and held in the refrigerator up to 24 hours.

¾ cup granulated sugar
2 teaspoons fresh lemon juice
1 teaspoon vanilla extract
¼ teaspoon salt
2 large eggs
2 large egg whites

6 ounces cake flour
 (about 1½ cups)
½ cup unsalted butter, melted
 and cooled
Baking spray with flour
3 tablespoons powdered sugar

1. Combine first 6 ingredients in a large bowl. Beat with a mixer at medium speed 5 minutes or until thick and pale. Weigh or lightly spoon flour into dry measuring cups; level with a knife. Sift flour over egg mixture, ½ cup at a time, folding in after each addition. Fold in butter. Cover and refrigerate 1 hour.

2. Preheat oven to 350°.

3. Fill shallow molds coated with baking spray two-thirds full. Bake at 350° for 8 minutes or until golden around edges. Cool in pan on a wire rack 2 minutes. Remove from pan, and cool completely on wire rack. Sift powdered sugar over cookies.

SERVES 18 (serving size: 2 cookies)
CALORIES 127; FAT 5.7g (sat 3.4g, mono 1.5g, poly 0.3g); PROTEIN 2g; CARB 17g; FIBER 0g; CHOL 34mg; IRON 1mg; SODIUM 47mg; CALC 6mg

PIPING COOKIES

1. These light batter cookies can be made in any shallow mold you have. Craft stores and sometimes local grocery stores offer loads of shapes and sizes in shallow molded pans for every holiday.

2. Using a plastic piping bag or a large zip-top plastic bag to pipe the batter into the molds keeps the molds and the cookies neat. Fill the molds two-thirds full with batter to leave a little room for the cookies to expand.

3. Let the cookies stand in the pan for 2 to 3 minutes after baking. This allows them to set up a bit so they don't fall apart when you remove them. Use a small offset spatula or a butter knife to gently remove them from the molds.

OATMEAL JUMBLES

Hands-on: 13 min. Total: 24 min.

Short on time but need a quick dessert? These jumble cookies come together in an instant and include whole-wheat flour and whole-grain oats for an earthy flavor and additional nutrition. Try substituting dried cranberries for the raisins for a sweet-tart variation.

½ cup quick-cooking oats
⅓ cup packed dark brown sugar
2 tablespoons unsalted butter, melted
1 tablespoon canola oil
½ teaspoon vanilla extract
1 large egg, lightly beaten
1.1 ounces all-purpose flour (about ¼ cup)
1 ounce whole-wheat flour (about ¼ cup)
½ teaspoon ground cinnamon
⅛ teaspoon baking soda
⅛ teaspoon baking powder
⅛ teaspoon salt
2 tablespoons chopped walnuts
2 tablespoons semisweet chocolate chips
2 tablespoons raisins

1. Preheat oven to 350°.

2. Combine first 6 ingredients in a large bowl; stir with a whisk until well combined. Weigh or lightly spoon flours into dry measuring cups; level with a knife. Add flours and next 4 ingredients (through salt) to sugar mixture; stir until just combined. Stir in nuts, chips, and raisins.

3. Drop dough by heaping tablespoons 2 inches apart (you should have 8 cookies) onto a baking sheet covered with parchment paper. Bake at 350° for 11 minutes or until just set. Cool on pan 1 minute. Cool on a wire rack.

SERVES 8 (serving size: 1 cookie)
CALORIES 158; FAT 7.7g (sat 2.8g, mono 2.8g, poly 1.6g); PROTEIN 3g; CARB 21g; FIBER 1g; CHOL 31mg; IRON 1mg; SODIUM 74mg; CALC 18mg

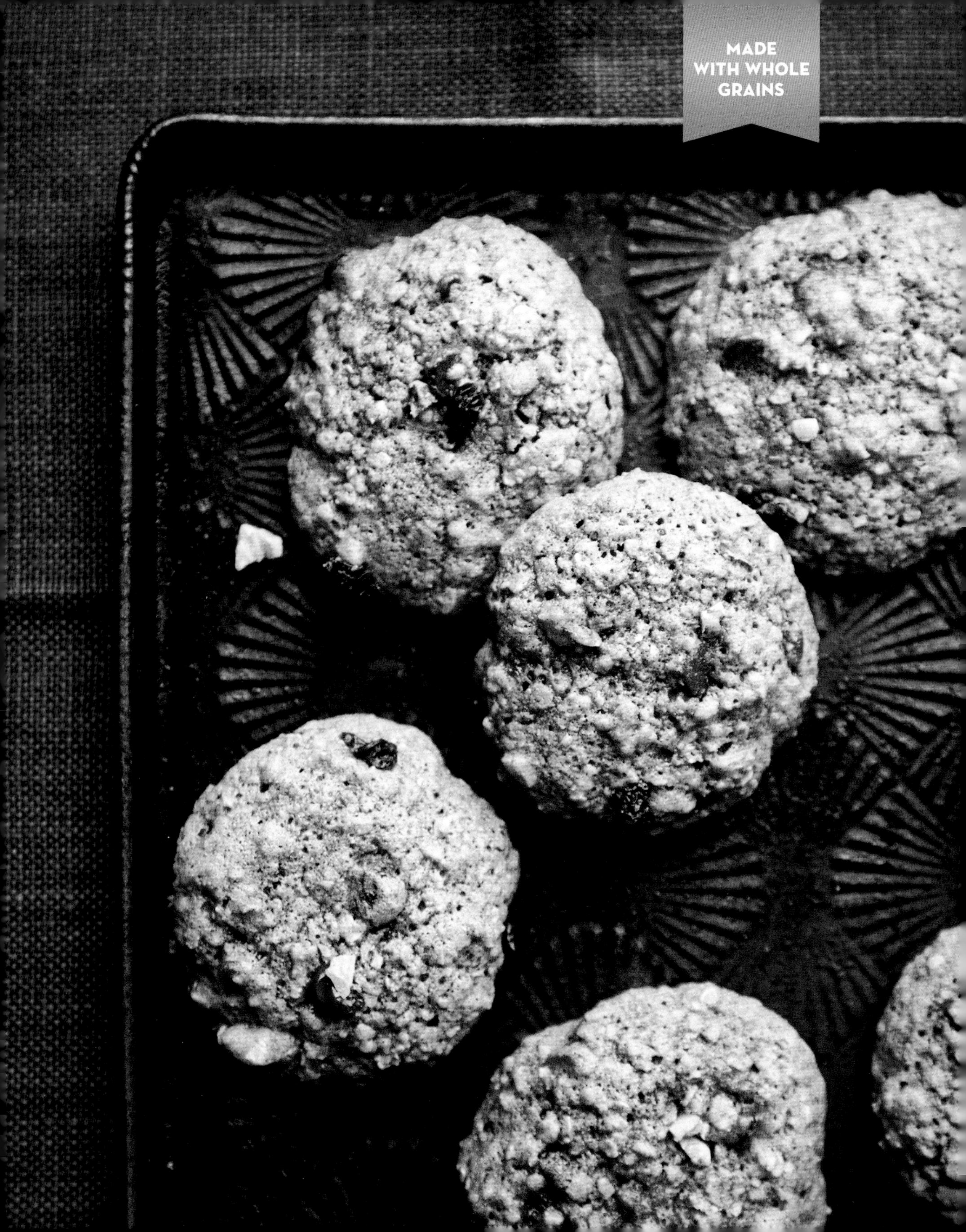
MADE
WITH WHOLE
GRAINS

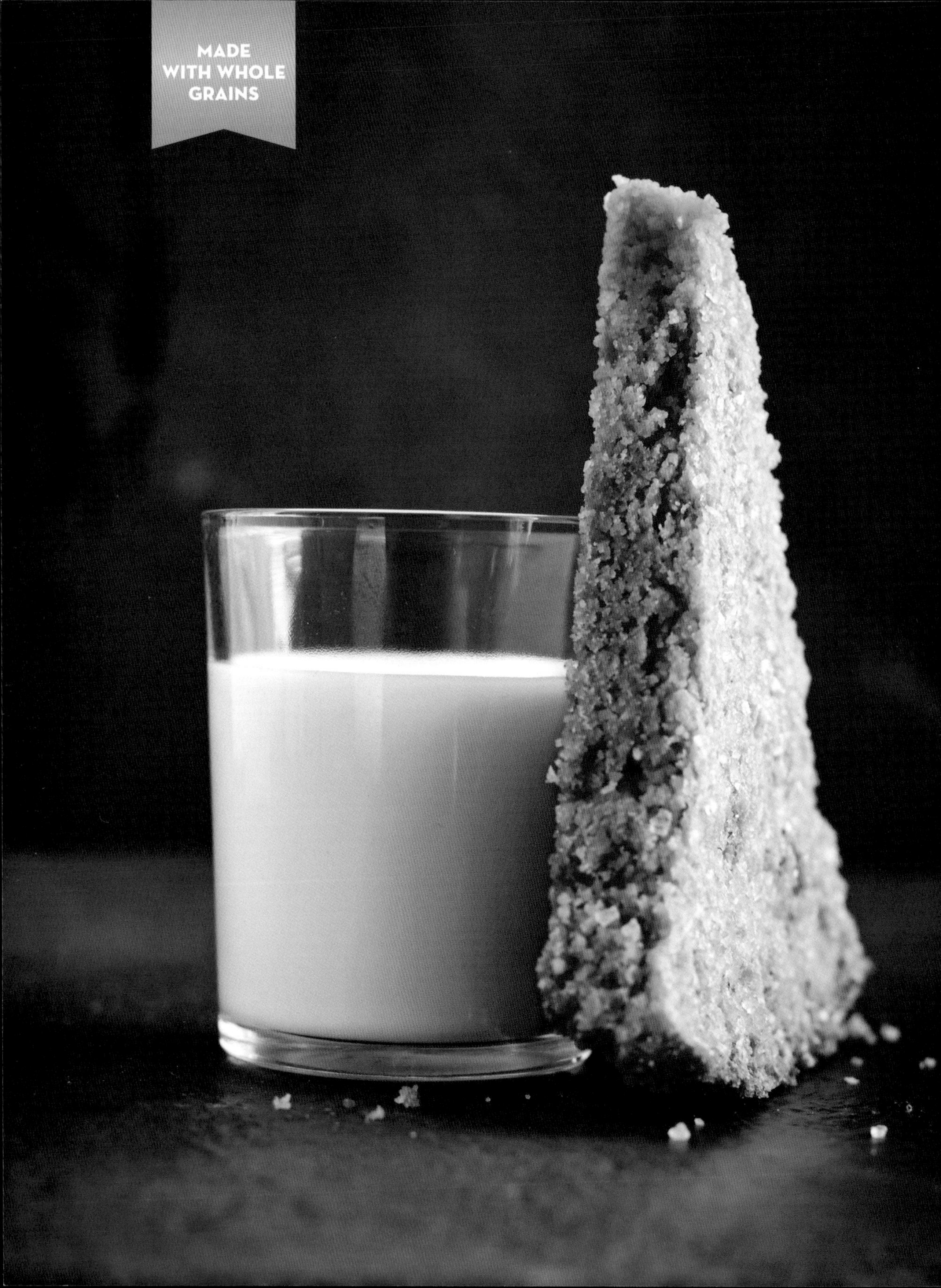
MADE
WITH WHOLE
GRAINS

SHORTBREAD COOKIE WEDGIES

Hands-on: 17 min. Total: 67 min.

The texture of Kamut adds substantial body without the doughy denseness you can get from regular whole-wheat flour.

4 ounces Kamut flour
  (about ⅔ cup)
3 ounces all-purpose flour (about
  ⅔ cup)
⅓ cup granulated sugar
⅓ cup packed brown sugar
3 tablespoons cornstarch
2 teaspoons grated orange rind
¼ teaspoon salt

¼ teaspoon baking powder
5 tablespoons unsalted butter,
  chilled
2 teaspoons vanilla extract
1 large egg
1 large egg yolk
Baking spray with flour
1 tablespoon sparkling sugar

1. Preheat oven to 325°.

2. Weigh or lightly spoon flours into dry measuring cups; level with a knife. Place flours and next 6 ingredients (through baking powder) in a food processor; process until well combined. Cut butter into ½-inch pieces; add to processor. Pulse 4 to 5 times or until mixture looks sandy. Combine vanilla, egg, and egg yolk in a small bowl; lightly beat with a fork. Add egg mixture to flour mixture; pulse 5 to 6 times or until just combined (do not overpulse or mixture will clump). Sprinkle mixture into a 9-inch springform pan coated with baking spray. Gently press mixture into bottom of pan. Sprinkle top with sparkling sugar.

3. Bake at 325° for 25 minutes or until lightly browned around edges. Cool in pan 10 minutes on a wire rack. Remove sides from pan; cool completely on wire rack. Remove from pan, and cut into 10 wedges.

SERVES 10 (serving size: 1 wedgie)
CALORIES 192; FAT 6.9g (sat 4g, mono 1.9g, poly 0.4g); PROTEIN 3g;
CARB 30g; FIBER 1g; CHOL 52mg; IRON 1mg; SODIUM 79mg; CALC 21mg

TECHNIQUE TIP

Baking at a lower temperature than usual (325° vs. 350°) allows for a longer baking time which ensures that the center gets done without drying out the cookie.

STAR ANISE AND ALMOND BISCOTTI

Add 2 teaspoons finely ground star anise to flour mixture. Omit pistachios and cherries. Stir in ¾ cup chopped roasted almonds.

SERVES 22 (serving size: 1 biscotto) CALORIES 119; FAT 3.2g (sat 0.4g); SODIUM 72mg

DARK CHOCOLATE CHIP BISCOTTI

Increase vanilla extract to 2 teaspoons. Omit pistachios and cherries. Stir in ½ cup coarsely chopped dark chocolate chips.

SERVES 22 (serving size: 1 biscotto) CALORIES 116; FAT 2.3g (sat 1.3g); SODIUM 74mg

ICED GINGERBREAD BISCOTTI

Add 3 tablespoons all-purpose flour, 1½ teaspoons ground cinnamon, 1 teaspoon ground ginger, and ½ teaspoon ground cloves to flour mixture. Increase vanilla extract to 2 teaspoons and add 2 tablespoons molasses to sugar mixture. Omit pistachios and cherries. To prepare icing, combine ⅔ cup powdered sugar, 1 tablespoon milk, and ¼ teaspoon vanilla extract; stir with a whisk until smooth. Spread icing on top of cooled biscotti.

SERVES 22 (serving size: 1 biscotto) CALORIES 115; FAT 0.8g (sat 0.2g); SODIUM 73mg

PISTACHIO AND TART CHERRY BISCOTTI

Hands-on: 30 min. Total: 1 hr. 50 min.

Twice-baked cookies are crisp and great for dunking. Leaving out butter or canola oil makes these biscotti extra crunchy. Be sure to let the cookie loaves cool after the first bake so they slice cleanly and don't crumble.

1 cup sugar
1 teaspoon vanilla extract
3 large eggs, divided
5.3 ounces whole-wheat pastry flour (about 1¼ cups)
4.5 ounces all-purpose flour (about 1 cup)
½ teaspoon salt
½ teaspoon baking powder
¾ cup roasted and lightly salted pistachios, chopped
¾ cup dried tart cherries, chopped

1. Preheat oven to 325°.

2. Place sugar, vanilla, and 2 eggs in a large bowl of a stand mixer; mix at high speed until ribbons fall from beaters, about 6 minutes.

3. Weigh or lightly spoon flours into dry measuring cups; level with a knife. Combine flours, salt, and baking powder in a bowl; stir with a whisk. Add flour mixture to egg mixture; mix at low speed until just combined. Stir in pistachios and cherries. Divide dough in half; place halves on a baking sheet covered with parchment paper. With lightly floured hands, shape each half into an 8 x 4–inch loaf. Lightly beat remaining egg in a bowl; brush tops and sides of loaves with egg. Bake at 325° for 35 minutes or until golden brown. Remove loaves from baking sheet, and cool 10 minutes on a wire rack.

4. Reduce oven temperature to 275°.

5. Cut each loaf diagonally into 11 (½-inch) slices; place slices, cut sides down, on baking sheet. Bake at 275° for 20 minutes, turning slices over after 10 minutes. Remove from pan, and cool completely on wire rack. Store biscotti in an airtight container.

SERVES 22 (serving size: 1 biscotto)
CALORIES 134; FAT 2.9g (sat 0.5g, mono 0.2g, poly 0.1g); PROTEIN 3g; CARB 24g; FIBER 3g; CHOL 21mg; IRON 1mg; SODIUM 83mg; CALC 17mg

CINNAMON-HONEY CRACKERS

Hands-on: 25 min. Total: 1 hr. 10 min.

Because I wanted these crackers to be similar to graham crackers, I blended the amaranth with all-purpose flour and added a touch of baking powder. This combo creates flat, crispy layers; pierce them with a fork to keep them from rising. The dough can be cut into any shape you like. Be sure to use very little flour on your work surface—too much flour worked into the dough can make the crackers dry. Reroll the scraps just one time. Any more than that will yield tough crackers.

AMARANTH

Amaranth is actually the seeds from a leafy plant and referred to as a pseudo-cereal. Packed with nutrients, amaranth is gluten free and a great way to include ancient-grain flavor in baked goods. Enjoy whole amaranth cooked into breakfast porridge or gently popped and mixed with nuts and coated with honey.

6.75 ounces all-purpose flour (about 1½ cups)
2.4 ounces amaranth flour (about ½ cup)
2 teaspoons ground cinnamon, divided
¼ teaspoon baking powder
¼ teaspoon baking soda
¼ teaspoon salt
½ cup unsalted butter
⅓ cup packed dark brown sugar
3 tablespoons honey
2 tablespoons canola oil
1 teaspoon vanilla extract
3 tablespoons granulated sugar

1. Weigh or lightly spoon flours into dry measuring cups; level with a knife. Combine flours, 1½ teaspoons cinnamon, baking powder, baking soda, and salt in a bowl; stir with a whisk.

2. Place butter in a medium bowl; beat with a mixer at medium speed until smooth. Add brown sugar, honey, oil, and vanilla; beat at medium speed until well combined. Add flour mixture; beat at low speed until just combined. Wrap dough in plastic wrap, and chill 30 minutes.

3. Preheat oven to 350°.

4. Place dough between 2 (16 x 12–inch) sheets of parchment paper. Roll dough to a 14 x 10–inch rectangle about ¼ inch thick. Remove and discard top parchment. Using a knife or pizza wheel, score dough into 20 crackers. (You'll cut all the way through the dough, but don't separate the crackers.) Using the tines of a fork, poke holes in center of each cracker. Place dough (on bottom parchment) on a baking sheet. (They are transferred as a whole piece.) Combine ½ teaspoon cinnamon and granulated sugar. Sprinkle top of dough evenly with mixture. Bake at 350° for 16 minutes or until browned.

SERVES 20 (serving size: 1 cracker)
CALORIES 131; FAT 6.4g (sat 3.1g, mono 2.1g, poly 0.6g); PROTEIN 2g; CARB 17g; FIBER 1g; CHOL 12mg; IRON 1mg; SODIUM 53mg; CALC 16mg

CHOCOLATE CHIP CREAM PUFFS

Hands-on: 45 min. Total: 2 hr.

At about half the calories of a pastry shop's version, these cream-filled puffs will amaze you. They're crisp and buttery with a creamy vanilla filling and glossy dark chocolate topping. I like to stir the chocolate chips into the warm batter by hand because the power of the mixer will incorporate the melting chips into the batter, making it chocolate batter instead of batter studded with chocolate chips. Baking the puffs on doubled sheet pans prevents burned bottoms.

PASTRY:
3/4 cup water
6 tablespoons unsalted butter
1 tablespoon granulated sugar
1/4 teaspoon salt
3.4 ounces all-purpose flour (about 3/4 cup)
2 large eggs
1 large egg white
1/2 cup semisweet chocolate chips

FILLING:
1 cup half-and-half
1/3 cup granulated sugar, divided
Dash of salt
2 tablespoons cornstarch
1 large egg
2 large egg yolks
1 tablespoon unsalted butter
1 teaspoon vanilla extract
1 cup frozen reduced-calorie whipped topping, thawed

GLAZE:
2 tablespoons light-colored corn syrup
1 tablespoon half-and-half
1 teaspoon vanilla extract
3/4 cup powdered sugar
2 tablespoons unsweetened cocoa

1. Preheat oven to 375°.

2. To prepare pastry, combine first 4 ingredients in a medium saucepan; bring to a boil. Weigh or lightly spoon flour into dry measuring cups; level with a knife. Add flour all at once to pan; stir with a wooden spoon until mixture pulls away from sides of pan and leaves a film on the bottom of the pan (about 3 minutes).

3. Spoon batter into a medium bowl. Beat with a mixer at medium speed 2 minutes or until mixture cools to about 120°. Add eggs and egg white, 1 at a time, beating at medium-low speed after each addition until completely combined (mixture will look lumpy but will get smooth quickly). Beat at medium speed 1 minute or until well combined. Stir in chocolate chips by hand. Drop about 2 tablespoons dough 2 inches apart onto doubled sheet pans covered with parchment paper (you will have 20 puffs). Bake at 375° for 20 minutes.

4. Reduce oven temperature to 325°. Rotate pans, and bake at 325° for an additional 25 minutes or until browned and crisp. Remove pans from oven. Pierce top of each puff with the tip of a knife. Cool completely on pans.

5. To prepare filling, combine 1 cup half-and-half, 3 tablespoons sugar, and dash of salt in a saucepan; bring to a simmer. Combine 2½ tablespoons sugar, cornstarch, egg, and egg yolks in a medium bowl; stir with a whisk until smooth. Gradually drizzle milk mixture into egg mixture, stirring constantly with a whisk. Return mixture to pan. Cook over medium heat until mixture thickens (about 4 minutes), stirring constantly.

6. Remove pan from heat; add butter and 1 teaspoon vanilla, stirring until smooth. Spoon cream into a medium bowl; place bowl in a large ice-filled bowl. Cool cream completely, stirring occasionally (about 20 minutes). Gently fold in whipped topping.

7. To prepare glaze, combine corn syrup, 1 tablespoon half-and-half, and 1 teaspoon vanilla in a microwave-safe bowl. Microwave at HIGH 15 seconds. Add powdered sugar and cocoa; stir with a whisk until smooth (glaze will be very thick and sticky).

8. To assemble cream puffs, cut the tops off the cooled puffs. Fill each puff with about 1 tablespoon pastry cream. Dip the tops in glaze, and place on top of filled cream puff.

SERVES 20 (serving size: 1 cream puff)
CALORIES 160; FAT 8.5g (sat 5.1g, mono 2.4g, poly 0.5g); PROTEIN 3g;
CARB 19g; FIBER 1g; CHOL 62mg; IRON 1mg; SODIUM 61mg; CALC 27mg

MY TOP 5 TIPS FOR
MAKING CREAM PUFFS

The French name for the pastry shell used in cream puffs, éclairs, and more filled desserts is pâte à choux (pronounced "pat ah shoe"). Fun to make and even more fun to eat, the batter is easily used in savory applications, too. Just omit the sugar in the batter, and fill the baked shells with herbed cream cheese, or make them into vessels to hold homemade chicken potpie filling.

1 *Be sure to cook the batter in a large saucepan so that you will have plenty of room for vigorous stirring. You will know when the batter is fully cooked when it leaves a fine film on the bottom of the pan.*

2 *It's very important to let the batter cool a bit before adding the eggs so you don't end up with bits of cooked egg in the puff. Add the eggs 1 at a time and only after each one is fully incorporated—the batter looks lumpy and slick until the egg gets fully combined. You want the batter as smooth and creamy as possible.*

3 *Portion the batter onto the parchment paper however you are most comfortable. Using piping bags, a small ice-cream scoop, or dropping by a tablespoon all work equally well. Be sure to double-up your baking pans. The puffs have to bake at a higher temperature to get crispy, but you don't want the bottoms getting too brown. Doubling up the pans helps insulate the puffs and prevents dark brown bottoms.*

4 *As soon as the puffs are removed from the oven, use the tip of a sharp knife to make a small slit in the top. This releases the steam from the inside and makes the puff crisper.*

5 *Use a serrated knife to cut off the top one-third of the puff. You'll get a cleaner cut, making for a prettier puff.*

FUDGE BROWNIE POPS

Hands-on: 30 min. Total: 1 hr. 20 min.

Incredibly moist and fudgy, these dark chocolate brownie pops studded with roasted almonds are decadent.

3 ounces bittersweet chocolate, divided
¼ cup unsalted butter
1 cup sugar
1 teaspoon vanilla extract
1 large egg
1 large egg white
3.4 ounces all-purpose flour (about ¾ cup)
½ cup unsweetened cocoa
½ teaspoon baking powder
¼ teaspoon baking soda
¼ teaspoon salt
Cooking spray
2 tablespoons dark corn syrup
16 lollipop sticks
½ cup roasted almonds, finely chopped

1. Preheat oven to 350°.

2. Finely chop 2 ounces chocolate; place in a medium microwave-safe bowl. Add butter to bowl. Microwave at HIGH 30 seconds or until mixture melts, stirring after 15 seconds. Add sugar, vanilla, egg, and egg white, stirring until well combined.

3. Weigh or lightly spoon flour into dry measuring cups; level with a knife. Combine flour and next 4 ingredients (through salt) in a bowl, stirring with a whisk. Add flour mixture to chocolate mixture, stirring until just combined. Scrape batter into an 8-inch square metal baking pan coated with cooking spray. Bake at 350° for 20 minutes or until a wooden pick inserted in center comes out clean. Cool completely in pan.

4. Crumble brownies in a food processor; process into fine crumbs. Add corn syrup; process until mixture forms a ball. Scoop about 2 tablespoons mixture, and shape into a ball; repeat procedure with remaining dough (you'll end up with 16 balls). Insert lollipop sticks into balls.

5. Finely chop 1 ounce chocolate; place in a microwave-safe bowl. Microwave at HIGH 30 seconds or until chocolate melts, stirring after 15 seconds. Dip balls into melted chocolate, and then into chopped nuts, pressing nuts to adhere. Refrigerate until chocolate sets, about 20 minutes.

SERVES 16 (serving size: 1 brownie pop)
CALORIES 170; FAT 8.3g (sat 3.5g, mono 2.5g, poly 0.8g); PROTEIN 3g;
CARB 24g; FIBER 2g; CHOL 19mg; IRON 1mg; SODIUM 113mg; CALC 28mg

TECHNIQUE TIP

For easier handling, stick the finished pop sticks into a block of Styrofoam, standing upright. Place the Styrofoam block with the pops into the refrigerator to chill and set.

TRIPLE HAZELNUT TRUFFLES

Hands-on: 20 min. Total: 1 hr. 20 min.

You'll find a triple hit of hazelnut goodness in these creamy two-bite truffles: hazelnut liqueur, chocolate-hazelnut spread, and toasted salted hazelnuts. Eating just one of these über rich chocolate bites will leave you satisfied.

5 ounces milk chocolate, finely chopped

3 tablespoons chocolate-hazelnut spread (such as Nutella)

2½ tablespoons hazelnut-flavored liqueur (such as Frangelico)

1 tablespoon light-colored corn syrup

½ teaspoon vanilla extract

⅓ cup finely chopped salted hazelnuts, toasted

1. Combine first 5 ingredients in a medium microwave-safe bowl. Microwave at HIGH 1 minute or until chocolate melts, stirring every 15 seconds. Spread mixture in the bottom of a shallow dish. Cover and refrigerate 1 hour or until set. Scoop about 2½ teaspoons chocolate mixture with a spoon (if chocolate is too firm to scoop, let it stand 5 to 10 minutes); roll into balls. Spread nuts in a single layer on wax paper; roll chocolate in nuts, pressing to adhere.

SERVES 18 (serving size: 1 truffle)
CALORIES 78; FAT 4.5g (sat 2.4g, mono 1g, poly 0.2g); PROTEIN 1g; CARB 9g; FIBER 1g; CHOL 0mg; IRON 0mg; SODIUM 8mg; CALC 17mg

THAI CASHEW BRITTLE

Hands-on: 35 min. Total: 2 hr. 35 min.

Sweet and spicy, this brittle combines the best of Thai cooking: lemongrass, chile paste, and fresh ginger. Cooking the sugar mixture to the stated temperature (335°) will give you lightly caramelized and crunchy brittle. Cooking to a lower temperature risks sticky, teeth-pulling candy. Be sure to coat your tools and parchment paper with cooking spray to help prevent sticking. Oh, and don't bother making this hard candy on a humid or rainy day; it just won't get hard and is guaranteed to stick to your teeth.

Cooking spray
2 cups sugar
1 cup light-colored corn syrup
½ cup water
1 cup coarsely chopped
   dry-roasted cashews, salted
1 tablespoon butter, softened
1 tablespoon chile paste
   (such as sambal oelek)

1 teaspoon baking soda
1 teaspoon grated fresh
   lemongrass (light green
   parts only)
1 teaspoon grated peeled
   fresh ginger

1. Line a baking sheet with parchment paper; coat lightly with cooking spray.

2. Combine sugar, corn syrup, and ½ cup water in a large heavy saucepan over medium-high heat, stirring just until combined; bring to a boil. Cook, without stirring, until a candy thermometer registers 335°. Remove pan from heat; stir in cashews and remaining ingredients (mixture will bubble). Pour mixture onto prepared pan, spreading it quickly and evenly with a spatula coated with cooking spray. Cool completely (about 2 hours); break into pieces.

SERVES 24 (serving size: 1 piece)
CALORIES 145; FAT 3.3g (sat 0.8g, mono 1.7g, poly 0.5g); PROTEIN 1g;
CARB 30g; FIBER 0g; CHOL 1mg; IRON 0mg; SODIUM 116mg; CALC 5mg

BRITTLE BASICS

1. It's very important to have all the ingredients prepared and ready to be stirred into the sugar syrup as soon as it's ready. Delaying allows the syrup to thicken, making it impossible to stir in the flavor ingredients.

2. Work fast to spread the brittle onto the prepared surface. It cools quickly, which can make it difficult to spread into a thin layer, so work quickly.

3. Allow the candy to cool completely before breaking it: You will be able to get more consistently sized pieces.

OLD SCHOOL

STONE FRUIT COBBLER

Hands-on: 17 min. Total: 67 min.

A cobbler is the ideal dessert to make with those end-of-the-season fruits that are very ripe, very soft, and very flavorful because you don't need the fruit to look pretty. It just needs to be juicy to exude all that luscious syrup to marry with the biscuit topping. You can do the topping two ways: Either completely cover the fruit by rolling the dough on a lightly floured surface, or leave openings between scoops to allow the fruit's juices to bubble up onto the biscuits. Both are delicious.

FILLING:

1 pound nectarines, pitted
   and quartered
1 pound ripe apricots, pitted
   and quartered
3/4 pound ripe plums, pitted
   and quartered
1/2 cup sugar
3 tablespoons cornstarch
1/2 teaspoon freshly ground
   nutmeg
1/4 teaspoon salt
Cooking spray

2 tablespoons unsalted butter,
   diced

TOPPING:

6.75 ounces all-purpose flour
   (about 1 1/2 cups)
2 tablespoons sugar
1 1/2 teaspoons baking powder
1/4 teaspoon salt
3 tablespoons chilled unsalted
   butter, cut into pieces
3/4 cup 2% reduced-fat milk
2 teaspoons sugar

1. Preheat oven to 350°.

2. To prepare filling, place first 3 ingredients in a large bowl. Combine 1/2 cup sugar, cornstarch, nutmeg, and salt in a small bowl. Add sugar mixture to fruit; toss gently to combine. Spoon mixture into an 11 x 7–inch glass or ceramic baking dish coated with cooking spray. Scatter diced butter over top of fruit mixture.

3. To prepare topping, weigh or lightly spoon flour into dry measuring cups; level with a knife. Combine flour, 2 tablespoons sugar, baking powder, and salt in a bowl; cut in butter with a pastry blender or 2 knives until mixture resembles small peas. Add milk to flour mixture; toss with a fork just until combined. Drop 12 heaping tablespoonfuls of dough onto fruit mixture. Sprinkle tops of dough evenly with 2 teaspoons sugar. Bake on lower rack of oven at 350° for 50 minutes or until biscuits are golden and fruit is bubbly.

SERVES 12 (serving size: about 2/3 cup)
CALORIES 205; FAT 5.7g (sat 3.3g, mono 1.6g, poly 0.4g); PROTEIN 3g;
CARB 37g; FIBER 2g; CHOL 14mg; IRON 1mg; SODIUM 167mg; CALC 65mg

TECHNIQUE TIP

To vary the flavor of this cobbler, feel free to choose any stone fruit you love, keeping the quantity about the same. Cherries, white and yellow nectarines, and peaches come in so many varieties, so it's easy to get creative in how you pack this simple dessert with fruit.

WHITE PEACH CRISP

Hands-on: 25 min. Total: 1 hr. 10 min.

Crisps and crumbles are basically the same dessert. What's wonderful about them is that they're quick and easy to make: There's no rolling, no chilling the dough. Plus, they're a good way to enjoy pie-like desserts with in-season fruit and a crumbly topping that get beautifully browned and crisp as they bake.

PEACHES

White peach season passes quickly, so keep your eyes open in the early summer to find ripe ones. Peel the peaches over a bowl to catch any juice drippings; add the juices back to the filling. Safeguard your oven by placing a piece of foil on the rack below the crisp to catch any juices that bubble over.

FILLING:
2½ pounds ripe white peaches, peeled and each cut into 6 wedges
¼ cup granulated sugar
1½ tablespoons all-purpose flour
¼ teaspoon salt
Cooking spray
2 tablespoons unsalted butter, diced

TOPPING:
1.5 ounces all-purpose flour (about ⅓ cup)
½ cup old-fashioned rolled oats
¼ cup packed brown sugar
½ teaspoon ground cinnamon
¼ teaspoon salt
3 tablespoons unsalted butter, melted

1. Preheat oven to 350°.

2. To prepare filling, combine peaches, granulated sugar, 1½ tablespoons flour, and salt in a large bowl; toss gently to combine. Spoon mixture into an 11 x 7–inch glass or ceramic baking dish coated with cooking spray. Scatter diced butter over top of fruit mixture.

3. To prepare topping, weigh or lightly spoon flour into a dry measuring cup; level with a knife. Place flour and next 4 ingredients (through salt) in a bowl; toss to combine. Add melted butter; toss until mixture is moist and crumbly. Sprinkle topping over fruit. Bake at 350° for 45 minutes or until topping is golden and filling is bubbly. Serve warm or at room temperature.

SERVES 8 (serving size: ¾ cup)
CALORIES 213; FAT 8.2g (sat 4.7g, mono 2.2g, poly 0.6g); PROTEIN 3g;
CARB 35g; FIBER 3g; CHOL 19mg; IRON 1mg; SODIUM 149mg; CALC 19mg

PERSIMMON-APPLE BROWN BETTY

Hands-on: 35 min. Total: 1 hr. 25 min.

Classic Brown Betty has layers of fruit and toasted bread-crumbs mixed with sugar and butter that's baked until the fruit is tender and the breadcrumbs on top are browned.

6 ounces whole-wheat bread, torn

5 tablespoons unsalted butter, divided

2 tablespoons granulated sugar

3/4 teaspoon ground cinnamon

1 1/2 pounds apples, peeled and cut into 1/2-inch wedges

1 1/2 pounds ripe Fuyu persimmons, peeled and cut into 1/2-inch wedges

1 cup unsweetened apple juice

1/2 cup packed brown sugar

1 tablespoon fresh lemon juice

1 teaspoon vanilla extract

1/4 teaspoon salt

Baking spray with flour

1/2 cup powdered sugar

3 tablespoons heavy cream

2 tablespoons 1/3-less-fat cream cheese

1/2 teaspoon grated lemon rind

Dash of salt

1. Preheat oven to 350°.

2. Place bread in a food processor; pulse until large crumbs form (should yield about 3 cups of crumbs). Melt 3 tablespoons butter in a large skillet over medium heat. Add breadcrumbs to pan; cook 5 minutes or until lightly browned and crisp, stirring frequently. Cool completely. Place crumbs, granulated sugar, and cinnamon in a bowl; toss well to combine.

3. Combine apple, persimmon, apple juice, brown sugar, lemon juice, vanilla, and salt in a bowl; toss well.

4. Spoon one-third of apple mixture into an 11 x 7–inch glass or ceramic baking dish coated with baking spray. Sprinkle with one-third of breadcrumb mixture. Repeat process 2 more times, ending with crumbs on top. Melt 2 tablespoons butter; drizzle over top of crumbs. Bake at 350° for 50 minutes or until bubbly and browned. Place pan on a wire rack to cool.

5. Combine powdered sugar and remaining ingredients in a bowl, stirring with a whisk until smooth. Serve warm with a dollop of topping.

SERVES 10

CALORIES 270; FAT 8.9g (sat 5.2g, mono 2.3g, poly 0.6g); PROTEIN 3g; CARB 47g; FIBER 4g; CHOL 24mg; IRON 1mg; SODIUM 167mg; CALC 56mg

PERSIMMONS

The two common varieties of persimmons found in grocery stores are Fuyu and Hachiya. Hachiya are larger, oval, and taller. Fuyu are squatter and more tomato shaped. The difference in taste is dramatic, so be sure to use Fuyu persimmons, as they are sweet yet firm and bake well. Hachiya persimmons are full of tannin until they become overly ripe and very soft. If persimmons aren't available, substitute ripe pears.

MY TOP 5 TIPS FOR
MAKING COBBLERS
AND CRISPS

No-fuss cobblers and crisps make the most of ripe and juicy in-season fruit. There's no chilling or rolling of pie dough, only scooping on the sweet, tender biscuit topping or sprinkling on the buttery combination of nuts and oats.

1 *The best tool I have found for removing the tender skin of fresh fruit is a serrated peeler. It gently removes the thinnest skin, leaving all the sweet juicy flesh for your cobbler. It works great on tomatoes, too.*

2 *Be gentle when mixing together cobbler toppings. The more the dough is stirred, the tougher it will be. And be sure the butter is very cold when it is added.*

3 *For the best possible flavor, use in-season fruit. Most supermarkets have almost any fruit available all year, but that doesn't necessarily mean they taste great. The apples from South Africa in July simply can't compare with apples from the United States in October.*

4 *Fresh ripe fruit releases its juice as it cooks, making a syrupy filling that's sweet and flavorful. If your fruit seems a little dry because it's not at its season's best, add a little unsweetened apple juice. When making slumps or grunts, the stovetop cooked filling should provide enough liquid to submerge the dumplings at least halfway up their sides.*

5 *Be sure to leave space between the dumplings and toppings on cobblers and crisps so that the filling can bubble up and caramelize on the top—it adds a lot of yummy flavor. And don't forget to place foil on the rack below the cobblers to catch any spillage or overflow.*

BLUEBERRY BUCKLE

Hands-on: 14 min. Total: 42 min.

The buckle gets its name from the addition of the granola-type topping that makes the cake dip and rise (or buckle) on top as it bakes.

TOPPING:
3 tablespoons old-fashioned rolled oats
2 tablespoons granulated sugar
2 tablespoons brown sugar
1 tablespoon all-purpose flour
1/8 teaspoon salt
3 tablespoons unsalted butter, chilled
3 tablespoons chopped pecans

CAKE:
6.75 ounces all-purpose flour (about 1 1/2 cups)

1 1/2 teaspoons baking powder
1/4 teaspoon salt
3/4 cup granulated sugar
2 tablespoons unsalted butter, softened
2 tablespoons canola oil
1 large egg
1 teaspoon vanilla extract
1/2 cup whole milk
1 cup fresh blueberries
Baking spray with flour

1. Preheat oven to 350°.

2. To prepare topping, combine first 5 ingredients in a bowl; toss well. Cut in butter with a pastry blender or 2 knives until mixture is crumbly. Stir in nuts; refrigerate until ready to use.

3. To prepare cake, weigh or lightly spoon flour into dry measuring cups; level with a knife. Combine flour, baking powder, and salt in a medium bowl, stirring with a whisk.

4. Place sugar, 2 tablespoons softened butter, and canola oil in a bowl; beat with a mixer at medium speed 2 minutes or until light and fluffy. Add egg and vanilla; beat well. Add milk; beat well. Add flour mixture; beat until just combined. Stir in blueberries by hand. Scoop batter into an 8 x 8–inch glass or ceramic baking dish coated with baking spray.

5. Sprinkle topping evenly over top of cake. Bake at 350° for 28 to 30 minutes or until a wooden pick inserted in center comes out almost clean. Cool in pan on a wire rack. Serve warm or at room temperature.

SERVES 9

CALORIES 300; FAT 12.5g (sat 4.9g, mono 4.9g, poly 1.9g); PROTEIN 4g;
CARB 44g; FIBER 1g; CHOL 39mg; IRON 1mg; SODIUM 194mg; CALC 74mg

TECHNIQUE TIP
Stirring the fresh blueberries in by hand instead of using the mixer keeps the batter from turning blue, which would look gray after baking. The strength and speed of the mixer would crush the berries, releasing their colorful juice, so gentle hand mixing is the way to go.

1. Adding sugar and a bit of butter to the filling gives it a lovely syrupy consistency and richness.

2. The dumplings are gently simmered and steamed in the fruit juices until they are barely done.

3. Don't peek at the dumplings while they cook. Lifting the lid off the pan will cause the steam to escape and will result in a longer cooking time. Trust your ears: If the liquid sounds like it is boiling vigorously, lower the heat.

MIXED BERRY SLUMP
WITH RICOTTA DUMPLINGS

Hands-on: 12 min. Total: 40 min.

Slumps are a mix of fruit and sweet dumplings cooked entirely on the stovetop. Their name is attributed to the appearance of the dumplings, as they "slump" on the plate surrounded by the cooked fruit. Adding ricotta cheese makes these dumplings creamier than typical recipes.

FILLING:
6 cups mixed fresh berries (blueberries, blackberries, raspberries)
½ cup apple juice or cranberry juice
¼ cup sugar
2 tablespoons unsalted butter, melted
1 tablespoon all-purpose flour
1 tablespoon fresh lemon juice
¼ teaspoon salt

DUMPLINGS:
3 ounces all-purpose flour (about ⅔ cup)
3 tablespoons sugar
1 teaspoon grated lemon rind
½ teaspoon baking powder
¼ teaspoon salt
1 cup part-skim ricotta cheese
1 large egg, lightly beaten

1. To prepare filling, gently combine first 7 ingredients in a 10-inch skillet with straight sides over medium-high heat; bring to a boil, stirring often. Cover and simmer 10 minutes or until fruit is very soft and juicy.

2. To prepare dumplings, weigh or lightly spoon flour into dry measuring cups; level with a knife. Combine flour and next 4 ingredients (through salt) in a medium bowl, stirring with a whisk. Add ricotta and egg; stir just until combined. Drop 8 generous tablespoonfuls dumpling mixture onto fruit mixture. Cover and simmer 18 minutes or until a wooden pick inserted in center of dumplings comes out clean. To serve, place 1 dumpling in a shallow bowl, and ladle berries over top.

SERVES 8 (serving size: 1 dumpling and about ½ cup berry mixture)
CALORIES 222; FAT 6.5g (sat 3.6g, mono 1.8g, poly 0.6g); PROTEIN 7g; CARB 36g; FIBER 5g; CHOL 40mg; IRON 1mg, SODIUM 218mg; CALC 128mg

GINGER-PLUM GRUNT

Hands-on: 19 min. Total: 47 min.

Grunts get their oddball name from the sound the fruit topped with dumpling dough makes while cooking on top of the stove. While grunts and slumps are very similar, this grunt starts on the stovetop and finishes under the broiler to give the dumplings a golden brown glow.

FILLING:
2½ pounds ripe plums, pitted and quartered
⅓ cup granulated sugar
2 tablespoons finely chopped crystallized ginger
1 tablespoon fresh lemon juice
¼ teaspoon salt

TOPPING:
6.75 ounces all-purpose flour (about 1½ cups)
2 tablespoons brown sugar
1½ teaspoons baking powder
¼ teaspoon salt
¼ cup butter, divided
¾ cup whole milk

1. To prepare filling, combine first 5 ingredients in a 10-inch broiler-safe skillet with straight sides; bring to a boil over medium-high heat, stirring often. Cover, reduce heat, and simmer 8 to 10 minutes or until plums begin to soften and mixture slightly thickens.

2. To prepare topping, weigh or lightly spoon flour into dry measuring cups; level with a knife. Place flour, brown sugar, baking powder, and salt in a large bowl; stir with a whisk. Place 3 tablespoons butter in a microwave-safe bowl; microwave at HIGH 30 seconds or until butter melts. Add melted butter and milk to flour mixture; stir until just combined. Drop 8 generous tablespoonfuls dumpling mixture onto fruit mixture. Cover and simmer 18 minutes or until a wooden pick inserted in center of dumplings comes out clean.

3. Preheat broiler.

4. Melt 1 tablespoon butter. Brush butter on top of dumplings. Place pan 8 inches under broiler; broil 2 minutes or until golden brown. Serve warm or at room temperature.

SERVES 8

CALORIES 272; FAT 7.1g (sat 4.1g, mono 1.9g, poly 0.4g); PROTEIN 4g;
CARB 50g; FIBER 3g; CHOL 18mg; IRON 2mg; SODIUM 250mg; CALC 97mg

TECHNIQUE TIP

If your plums are not very juicy, you may need to add water or unsweetened apple juice to the simmering fruit to get enough liquid to cook the dumplings. The cooking liquid should be as thick as maple syrup and needs to come halfway up the sides of the dumplings when they are dropped in.

MOLASSES-APPLE PANDOWDY

Hands-on: 32 min. Total: 1 hr. 42 min.

Pandowdy is basically a single-crust fruit pie baked in a casserole dish. Breaking the top crust in the final 10 minutes of cooking is said to make the dish unattractive or "dowdy." Use a variety of apples for more interesting flavor and texture.

CRUST:
6.75 ounces all-purpose flour
   (about 1¼ cups)
¼ teaspoon baking powder
¼ teaspoon salt
3 tablespoons unsalted butter,
   cold
3 tablespoons natural shortening
   (such as Earth Balance)
4 tablespoons ice water
1½ teaspoons white vinegar

FILLING:
4 pounds apples, peeled and cut
   into ⅛-inch-thick slices

½ cup unsweetened apple
   juice
¼ cup molasses
¼ cup granulated sugar
¼ cup packed brown sugar
2 tablespoons cornstarch
1 teaspoon ground cinnamon
½ teaspoon ground ginger
¼ teaspoon salt
Baking spray with flour
3 tablespoons unsalted butter,
   diced
1 large egg white
2 tablespoons turbinado
   sugar

1. To prepare crust, weigh or lightly spoon flour into dry measuring cups; level with a knife. Place flour, baking powder, and salt in a food processor; process to combine.

2. Cut butter and shortening into ½-inch pieces; add to processor. Pulse 2 to 3 times or until butter is about the size of dried peas. Sprinkle ice water and vinegar over mixture; pulse 2 to 3 times or until mixture is combined and looks like coarse sand. (Do not overprocess mixture; the dough will become clumpy and tough.)

3. Scrape mixture onto a lightly floured work surface. Gather mixture together, and press into a 4-inch disc. Cover disc with plastic wrap, and chill 30 minutes.

4. Preheat oven to 425°.

5. To prepare filling, place apples and next 8 ingredients (through salt) in a large bowl; toss gently to combine. Spoon mixture into a 13 x 9–inch glass or ceramic baking dish coated with baking spray. Scatter diced butter over top.

6. Unwrap dough, and place on a lightly floured work surface. Roll to a 14 x 10–inch rectangle. Place dough on top of filling; tuck dough between filling and dish. Cut slits in top of dough to allow steam to escape. Place egg white in a small bowl; stir well with a whisk. Brush dough with egg white; sprinkle with turbinado sugar. Bake at 425° for 10 minutes; reduce oven temperature to 350°. Bake at 350° an additional 20 minutes or until golden and bubbly. Remove pie from oven. "Dowdy" the crust by breaking through the crust with the edge of a large spoon. Bake at 350° for an additional 10 minutes or until browned and bubbly. Serve warm or at room temperature.

SERVES 14

CALORIES 259; FAT 9.4g (sat 5.4g, mono 2.4g, poly 0.9g); PROTEIN 2g; CARB 43g; FIBER 2g; CHOL 13mg; IRON 1mg; SODIUM 92mg; CALC 27mg

RASPBERRY-BLUEBERRY CLAFOUTIS

Hands-on: 25 min. Total: 1 hr. 20 min.

I learned about this dessert (pronounced kla-foo-TEE) when I was in culinary school. The classic French dessert of tender cakey custard studded with fruit is easy to make. It traditionally contains cherries, but I opted to use colorful fresh berries.

2 ounces cake flour
   (about ½ cup)
½ cup granulated sugar
¼ teaspoon salt
3 large eggs
2 large egg yolks
⅔ cup whole milk
2 tablespoons unsalted butter,
   melted and cooled

¼ teaspoon vanilla extract
Baking spray with flour
1 (6-ounce) package fresh
   raspberries
½ cup blueberries
1 tablespoon powdered sugar

1. Preheat oven to 375°.

2. Weigh or lightly spoon flour into a dry measuring cup; level with a knife. Place flour, sugar, and salt in a large bowl; stir with a whisk. Add eggs and egg yolks; stir with whisk until combined. Stir in milk, butter, and vanilla.

3. Pour mixture into a blender; process until smooth. Pour mixture into a 9½-inch deep-dish pie plate coated with baking spray. Arrange berries on top of batter; do not stir. Bake at 375° for 35 minutes or until almost set in the middle. Let stand 20 minutes or until set before slicing. Sift powdered sugar over top.

SERVES 8 (serving size: 1 wedge)
CALORIES 183; FAT 8.1g (sat 4.1g, mono 2.5g, poly 0.8g); PROTEIN 5g;
CARB 24g; FIBER 1g; CHOL 129mg; IRON 1mg; SODIUM 111mg; CALC 46mg

TECHNIQUE TIP

Be careful not to overbake the clafoutis—pull it from the oven when the center still wiggles a bit. To serve, scoop it with a spoon while it's still warm, or slice it into wedges when it's completely cooled.

CRANBERRY-ORANGE RICE PUDDING

Decrease sugar to ¼ cup in rice mixture and ¼ cup in eggs. Decrease vanilla to ½ teaspoon. Remove from heat; stir in ½ teaspoon orange rind and ½ cup dried cranberries. Omit cinnamon or nutmeg.

SERVES 8 (serving size: about ½ cup) CALORIES 203; FAT 4g (sat 2g); SODIUM 149mg

RUM-RAISIN RICE PUDDING

Microwave ⅓ cup raisins and 3 tablespoons dark rum at HIGH 30 seconds. Let stand. Decrease vanilla to 1 teaspoon. Stir raisin mixture into pudding. Decrease cinnamon to ¼ teaspoon. Do not use nutmeg.

SERVES 8 (serving size: about ½ cup) CALORIES 229; FAT 3.9g (sat 2g); SODIUM 149mg

BRÛLÉED RICE PUDDING

At end of Step 2, divide pudding among 8 dessert bowls; cover with plastic wrap, pressing into top of pudding. Omit cinnamon. Chill 2 hours, until cold and firm. Sprinkle each pudding with 2 teaspoons sugar. Move a kitchen blow torch 2 inches above top of each pudding back and forth, until sugar is completely melted and caramelized (about 1 minute). Serve immediately.

SERVES 8 (serving size: about ½ cup) CALORIES 229; FAT 3.9g (sat 2g); SODIUM 149mg

RICE PUDDING

Hands-on: 69 min. Total: 69 min.

This is one of my childhood favorites—one my grandmother would have ready for an after-school snack. Her recipe was very simple, so this recipe is a tribute to her and the simple dessert that allows you to put a lot of different spins on it. Long, slow cooking makes for a creamy rice pudding. Using Arborio rice (typically used in risotto) ensures that the pudding will be smooth and yet still retain shape and texture. Sprinkle with toasted nuts, like pistachios or walnuts, if you like.

4 cups 2% reduced-fat milk
⅔ cup sugar, divided
½ cup Arborio rice
½ teaspoon salt

2 large eggs
1½ teaspoons vanilla extract
½ teaspoon ground cinnamon
or nutmeg

1. Combine milk, ⅓ cup sugar, rice, and salt in a large heavy-bottomed saucepan; bring to a simmer over medium heat. Cover, reduce heat, and simmer 45 minutes or until about one-fourth of liquid remains, stirring frequently.

2. Combine ⅓ cup sugar, eggs, and vanilla in a bowl; stir well with a whisk. Gradually add about 2 cups hot rice mixture to egg mixture, stirring constantly with a whisk. Slowly pour egg mixture back into pan, stirring constantly; cook 5 minutes or until mixture thickens, stirring constantly over medium-low heat.

3. Pour rice pudding into a serving dish; sprinkle top evenly with cinnamon. Serve warm or cold.

SERVES 8 (serving size: about ½ cup)
CALORIES 197; FAT 3.9g (sat 2g, mono 1.2g, poly 0.5g); PROTEIN 7g; CARB 34g; FIBER 0g; CHOL 56mg; IRON 0mg; SODIUM 149mg; CALC 156mg

MY TOP 5 TIPS FOR MAKING RICE PUDDING

While rice pudding may seem like a simple dessert, not following the cooking method and ingredient suggestions exactly may produce something closer to wallpaper paste.

1 *There are so many varieties of rice, and each variety lends its unique qualities to prepared dishes. I typically choose medium-grain Arborio rice when I'm making rice pudding because it becomes creamy and the grains will cling together rather than stay firm and separated, like long-grain rice used in fried rice dishes.*

2 *A ratio of 8-to-1 is the key to cooking the rice properly. Using 4 cups of milk to only ½ cup of rice may seem like a lot of liquid, but cooking the rice slowly in this much milk makes the rice superplump and creamy.*

3 *Tempering the eggs at the very end of cooking the rice makes the pudding creamier.*

4 *Vanilla extract is made with a large amount of alcohol, and if it is added too soon to hot liquids, it will evaporate and not be as flavorful as you want. Stir it in near the end of cooking to get the most flavor.*

5 *By all means, if you have a vanilla bean and enjoy the appearance of the tiny seeds, use it instead of adding the vanilla extract. Simply split the bean in half lengthwise, leaving one of the ends uncut, and then add the bean when you first start cooking the rice. Pluck the bean from the pudding just before scooping it into the serving bowl.*

CHOCOLATE PUDDING CAKE

Hands-on: 15 min. Total: 60 min.

Warm, gooey, and oh so chocolaty, this old-school dessert is just as tasty today as it was in the good old days.

4.5 ounces all-purpose flour
   (about 1 cup)
¾ cups granulated sugar, divided
¼ cup unsweetened cocoa,
   divided
2 teaspoons baking powder
¼ teaspoon salt
½ cup 2% reduced-fat milk
2 tablespoons unsalted butter,
   melted

1 teaspoon vanilla extract
Baking spray with flour
¼ cup packed brown sugar
1¼ cups strong hot coffee
9 tablespoons frozen reduced-
   calorie whipped topping
   (such as Cool Whip), thawed

1. Preheat oven to 350°.

2. Weigh or lightly spoon flour into a dry measuring cup; level with a knife. Combine flour, ½ cup sugar, 2 tablespoons cocoa, baking powder, and salt in a bowl, stirring with a whisk. Add milk, butter, and vanilla; stir until just combined. Scrape batter into a 9 x 9–inch metal baking pan coated with baking spray. Combine ¼ cup sugar, 2 tablespoons cocoa, and brown sugar; sprinkle mixture over top of batter. Carefully pour coffee over top (do not stir in).

3. Bake at 350° for 28 to 30 minutes or until just set (do not overbake). Let stand 10 minutes; top with whipped topping.

SERVES 9 (serving size: 1 piece and 1 tablespoon topping)
CALORIES 187; FAT 3.8g (sat 2.5g, mono 0.9g, poly 0.2g); PROTEIN 2g;
CARB 38g; FIBER 1g; CHOL 8mg; IRON 1mg; SODIUM 183mg; CALC 88mg

WWII RATION CAKE

Hands-on: 17 min. Total: 69 min.

Despite the name, this rich, intensely chocolate cake is anything but depressing. Here's a little history: During World War II many imported foods, such as sugar and coffee, were rationed. Transporting food across the nation almost came to a halt because gasoline and tires were diverted to military efforts. We owe a debt of gratitude to the crafty baker who developed this recipe using the ingredients on hand.

CAKE:
10.1 ounces all-purpose flour (about 2¼ cups)
1¼ cups granulated sugar
6 tablespoons unsweetened cocoa
1½ teaspoons baking soda
½ teaspoon salt
1½ cups cold water
½ cup canola oil
1½ tablespoons white vinegar
1 teaspoon vanilla extract
Baking spray with flour

ICING:
3 tablespoons 2% reduced-fat milk
2 tablespoons unsalted butter
2 cups powdered sugar, divided
2 tablespoons unsweetened cocoa
½ teaspoon vanilla extract
Dash of salt

1. Preheat oven to 350°.

2. To prepare cake, weigh or lightly spoon flour into dry measuring cups; level with a knife. Combine flour and next 4 ingredients (through salt) in a large bowl, stirring with a whisk.

3. Place 1½ cups cold water, oil, vinegar, and vanilla in a small bowl, stirring with a whisk. Add water mixture to flour mixture; stir until just combined (some small lumps will be in the batter). Scrape batter into a 13 x 9–inch metal baking pan coated with baking spray. Bake at 350° for 22 minutes or until a wooden pick inserted in center comes out with moist crumbs.

4. To prepare icing, place milk and butter in a medium microwave-safe bowl; microwave at HIGH 30 seconds or until butter melts. Reserve 1 tablespoon powdered sugar. Add remaining powdered sugar, cocoa, vanilla, and salt to milk mixture; stir until smooth. Spread icing over top of warm cake. Cool completely. Sift reserved 1 tablespoon powdered sugar over top of cake.

SERVES 15 (serving size: 1 piece)
CALORIES 286; FAT 9.6g (sat 1.8g, mono 5.3g, poly 2.3g); PROTEIN 3g;
CARB 49g; FIBER 1g; CHOL 4mg; IRON 1mg; SODIUM 216mg; CALC 11mg

TECHNIQUE TIP

Why are some cakes stirred together by hand while others are beaten with a mixer? It's all about the texture. Beating with a mixer incorporates air and makes a cake lighter and taller, while mixing by hand creates a moist, dense texture.

BANANA-NUT BREAD

Hands-on: 16 min. Total: 1 hr. 51 min.

Try toasting a slice of this banana bread and topping it with a scoop of fat-free vanilla ice cream. Yum!

6.75 ounces all-purpose flour
   (about 1½ cups)
½ teaspoon baking powder
½ teaspoon baking soda
½ teaspoon salt
6 tablespoons unsalted butter,
   at room temperature
1 cup granulated sugar
2 large eggs
1 cup ripe mashed banana
   (about 2 large)

1 teaspoon vanilla extract
½ cup reduced-fat sour cream
½ cup chopped pecans or
   walnuts, lightly toasted
Baking spray with flour
⅔ cup powdered sugar
2 teaspoons fresh lemon juice
2 teaspoons 2% reduced-fat milk

1. Preheat oven to 350°.

2. Weigh or lightly spoon flour into dry measuring cups; level with a knife. Combine flour, baking powder, baking soda, and salt in a bowl, stirring with a whisk.

3. Place butter in a large bowl; beat with a mixer at medium speed until smooth, about 1 minute. Add granulated sugar; beat 1 minute. Add eggs, 1 at a time, beating well after each addition. Beat in banana and vanilla until just combined. Add flour mixture alternately with sour cream, beginning and ending with flour mixture. Stir in nuts by hand. Scrape batter into a 9 x 5–inch loaf pan coated with baking spray. Bake at 350° for 50 minutes or until a wooden pick inserted in center comes out clean. Cool 10 minutes in pan on a wire rack. Remove from pan, and cool completely on wire rack.

4. Combine powdered sugar, lemon juice, and milk in a small bowl; stir with a whisk until smooth. Drizzle glaze over top and down sides of bread. Let stand 5 minutes before slicing.

SERVES 12 (serving size: 1 slice)
CALORIES 280; FAT 11.5g (sat 5.1g, mono 4.1g, poly 1.5g); PROTEIN 4g;
CARB 42g; FIBER 1g; CHOL 50mg; IRON 1mg; SODIUM 191mg; CALC 40mg

TECHNIQUE TIP

Since bananas are naturally sweet, I added lemon juice to the powdered sugar glaze just to give a bit of tartness and balance the sweetness. If you really like a tart bite, use all lemon juice in the glaze.

CHOCOLATE-ZUCCHINI BREAD

Hands-on: 25 min. Total: 1 hr. 50 min.

I remember zucchini bread from the early days of the health-food trend. It was greasy with vegetable oil and didn't have much flavor. My version is a big improvement. A bounty of shredded zucchini and molasses-y brown sugar make it moist; cocoa and chocolate chips make it decadent.

2 cups shredded zucchini (about ½ pound)
8 ounces all-purpose flour (about 1¾ cups)
7 tablespoons unsweetened cocoa, divided
1 teaspoon baking powder
½ teaspoon baking soda
¼ teaspoon salt
⅓ cup granulated sugar
¼ cup packed brown sugar
¼ cup unsalted butter, softened
¼ cup canola oil
1 teaspoon vanilla extract
2 large eggs
½ cup semisweet or dark chocolate chips
Baking spray with flour
½ cup powdered sugar
1 tablespoon 2% reduced-fat milk
Dash of salt

1. Preheat oven to 350°.

2. Place zucchini in a sieve; let stand 10 minutes, pressing down occasionally to release liquid.

3. Weigh or lightly spoon flour into dry measuring cups; level with a knife. Combine flour, 6 tablespoons cocoa, and next 3 ingredients (through salt) in a bowl, stirring with a whisk.

4. Place granulated sugar and next 4 ingredients (through vanilla) in a large bowl; beat with a mixer at medium speed until well combined, about 5 minutes. Add eggs, 1 at a time, beating well after each addition. Add flour mixture to sugar mixture; beat at low speed until just combined. Stir in chocolate chips and zucchini. Spoon batter into a 9 x 4–inch loaf pan coated with baking spray. Bake at 350° for 38 minutes or until a wooden pick inserted in center comes out clean. Cool in pan on a wire rack 15 minutes. Loosen edges from sides. Remove from pan, and cool completely on wire rack.

5. Combine powdered sugar, 1 tablespoon cocoa, milk, and dash of salt in a small bowl, stirring with a whisk until smooth. Drizzle glaze over top of loaf.

SERVES 12 (serving size: 1 slice)
CALORIES 260; FAT 12.1g (sat 4.6g, mono 5.1g, poly 1.8g); PROTEIN 4g; CARB 37g; FIBER 2g; CHOL 41mg; IRON 2mg; SODIUM 171mg; CALC 46mg

TECHNIQUE TIP

Be sure to press out the excess moisture from the shredded zucchini; otherwise, you will end up with a dense, gummy loaf of bread.

WHOLE-GRAIN APPLESAUCE BARS

Hands-on: 20 min. Total: 1 hr. 30 min.

Using applesauce in place of butter or oil is a diet trick that's as old as the hills. The upside is fewer calories; the downside is typically a dense, gummy baked good. In these bars, I've used less applesauce, added a little canola oil for tenderness, and included tons of old-fashioned oats to provide texture to the heavy whole-wheat flour.

4.75 ounces whole-wheat flour (about 1 cup)
2 tablespoons flaxseed meal (optional)
2 cups old-fashioned rolled oats
1 teaspoon ground cinnamon
½ teaspoon baking powder
½ teaspoon baking soda
½ teaspoon salt
2 large ripe bananas
¾ cup packed brown sugar
½ cup applesauce
2 tablespoons canola oil
1 teaspoon vanilla extract
1 large egg
1 large egg white
¾ cup chopped walnuts, lightly toasted
¾ cup dried cranberries
Baking spray with flour

1. Preheat oven to 350°.

2. Weigh or lightly spoon flour into a dry measuring cup; level with a knife. Combine flour, flaxseed, if desired, and next 5 ingredients (through salt) in a bowl; stir with a whisk.

3. Place bananas in a large bowl; mash with a fork or a potato masher until smooth. Add brown sugar and next 5 ingredients (through egg white); stir until well combined. Add flour mixture, stirring until combined. Stir in nuts and dried cranberries.

4. Spread dough into a 13 x 9–inch metal baking pan coated with baking spray. Bake at 350° for 20 to 22 minutes or until a wooden pick inserted in center comes out clean. Cool completely in pan on a wire rack. Cut into 16 bars.

SERVES 16 (serving size: 1 bar)
CALORIES 199; FAT 7.1g (sat 0.8g, mono 2.1g, poly 3.8g); PROTEIN 4g; CARB 32g; FIBER 3g; CHOL 12mg; IRON 1mg; SODIUM 139mg; CALC 32mg

TECHNIQUE TIP

If you prefer other dried fruit and nut combinations, feel free to substitute. Just use the same quantities for similar nutrition. Try dried apricots and hazelnuts, or almonds and dried cherries. How about dates and pistachios? Get creative!

DEVIL DOGS

Hands-on: 1 hr. Total: 1 hr. 28 min.

This recipe was inspired by Drake's Devil Dog bone-shaped snack cake popularized in the 1920s. My version is two moist devil's food cookies filled with gooey vanilla Swiss meringue.

1 ounce unsweetened chocolate, finely chopped
¼ cup canola oil
9 ounces all-purpose flour (about 2 cups)
½ cup unsweetened cocoa
1 teaspoon baking powder
¼ teaspoon baking soda
¼ teaspoon salt
¼ cup unsalted butter, softened
¾ cup packed brown sugar
¾ cup granulated sugar, divided
2 large eggs
2 teaspoons vanilla extract, divided
1 cup low-fat buttermilk
2 tablespoons light-colored corn syrup
¼ teaspoon cream of tartar
Dash of salt
2 large egg whites

1. Preheat oven to 350°.

2. Place chocolate and oil in a small microwave-safe bowl; microwave at HIGH 30 seconds or until chocolate melts. Stir, and cool completely.

3. Weigh or lightly spoon flour into dry measuring cups; level with a knife. Combine flour and next 4 ingredients, stirring with a whisk.

4. Place butter in a large bowl; beat with a mixer at medium speed 1 minute or until smooth. Add brown sugar and ¼ cup granulated sugar; beat 1 minute or until well combined. Add eggs, 1 at a time, beating well after each addition. Beat in chocolate mixture and 1 teaspoon vanilla. Add flour mixture and buttermilk alternately to chocolate mixture, beginning and ending with flour mixture. Drop by level tablespoonfuls 2 inches apart onto baking sheets covered with parchment paper. (You should have 52 cookies.) Bake at 350° for 8 minutes or just until set. Cool cookies on pans 4 minutes; remove from pans, and cool completely on wire racks.

5. Place ½ cup granulated sugar, corn syrup, cream of tartar, dash of salt, and egg whites in the top of a double boiler; stir with a whisk until combined. Cook mixture over simmering water about 3 minutes or until a candy thermometer registers 160°, stirring constantly with a whisk. Remove pan from heat. Beat with a mixer at high speed using clean, dry beaters about 8 minutes or until soft peaks form. Beat in 1 teaspoon vanilla. Spread about 1 tablespoon filling on bottom side of 1 cookie; top with another cookie. Repeat procedure with remaining cookies and filling.

SERVES 26 (serving size: 1 cookie sandwich)
CALORIES 143; FAT 5.3g (sat 2g, mono 2.3g, poly 0.8g); PROTEIN 3g;
CARB 23g; FIBER 1g; CHOL 19mg; IRON 1mg; SODIUM 90mg; CALC 34mg

CORN SYRUP

Adding corn syrup to Swiss meringue makes it creamy, glossy, and gooey. Corn syrup has a natural tendency to prevent other sugars from recrystallizing, a process that occurs in sugar-rich sauces like caramel and butterscotch and even in natural honey.

LEMON SYLLABUB

Hands-on: 7 min. Total: 67 min.

Kind of like thick and creamy eggnog, this boozy high-octane dessert originated in England during the Tudor era. Robert May's cookbook, The Accomplisht Cook (1685 edition) calls for cider, probably fermented. But I really liked the cookbook by Richard Briggs, The New Art of Cookery, According to the Present Practice (published in 1788) that calls for placing the spirits in a bowl and milking a cow directly into the bowl to help with the desired frothiness. If you don't have a cow, feel free to use your hand mixer. If the kids want to join in, simply make theirs by whipping cream and lemonade together and folding in the whipped topping.

6 ounces sweet white wine
  (such as Gewürztraminer)
6 tablespoons superfine sugar
6 tablespoons lemon liqueur
  (such as limoncello)
4 (1-inch) wide lemon rind strips

½ cup heavy whipping cream
¾ cup frozen reduced-calorie
  whipped topping (such as
  Cool Whip), thawed
2 lemon biscotti cookies, coarsely
  crushed

1. Place wine, sugar, liqueur, and lemon rind in a medium mixing bowl; stir until sugar dissolves. Chill 30 minutes.

2. Discard lemon rind. Add cream. Beat with a mixer at medium speed 4 minutes or until mixture slightly thickens. Gently fold in whipped topping. Divide mixture among 8 wine glasses. Chill 30 minutes.

3. Sprinkle tops of syllabub evenly with cookie crumbs. Serve immediately.

SERVES 8

CALORIES 185; FAT 7.6g (sat 4.8g, mono 1.7g, poly 0.2g); PROTEIN 1g; CARB 20g; FIBER 0g; CHOL 26mg; IRON 0mg; SODIUM 30mg; CALC 20mg

FROZEN
AND
CHILLED

TRIPLE CHOCOLATE CHEESECAKE

Hands-on: 25 min. Total: 14 hr.

⅔ cup old-fashioned rolled oats
4 chocolate graham cracker sheets (16 crackers)
2 tablespoons dark brown sugar
⅜ teaspoon salt, divided
1 tablespoon butter, melted
1 large egg white
Baking spray with flour
1 cup granulated sugar
¼ cup unsweetened cocoa
2 tablespoons cake flour
12 ounces fat-free cream cheese, softened
10 ounces ⅓-less-fat cream cheese, softened
4 large eggs, at room temperature
1 ounce bittersweet chocolate, melted and cooled
1 teaspoon vanilla extract
2 cups frozen reduced-calorie whipped topping (such as Cool Whip), thawed and divided
1 cup fresh raspberries

1. Preheat oven to 350°.

2. Spread oats on a baking sheet. Bake at 350° for 10 minutes, stirring after 5 minutes. Cool oats 10 minutes on pan. Place oats, crackers, brown sugar, and ⅛ teaspoon salt in a food processor; process until finely ground. Add melted butter and egg white; process until moist. Press mixture into bottom and 1½ inches up sides of a 9-inch springform pan coated with baking spray. Bake at 350° for 10 to 12 minutes or until toasted and fragrant. Cool completely on a wire rack.

3. Reduce oven temperature to 325°.

4. Sift together granulated sugar, cocoa, flour, and ¼ teaspoon salt in a bowl. Beat cream cheeses with a mixer at medium speed until smooth. Add eggs, 1 at a time, beating well after each addition. Add chocolate and vanilla, beating at low speed until just combined. Sprinkle sugar mixture over top of cheese mixture; beat at low speed until combined. Gently fold 1 cup whipped topping into mixture. Pour mixture into prepared pan, smoothing top. Bake at 325° for 1 hour or until cheesecake center barely moves when pan is touched.

5. Remove cheesecake from oven; run a knife around edge. Cool to room temperature. Cover and chill at least 8 hours. Serve with 1 cup whipped topping and berries.

SERVES 16 (serving size: 1 cheesecake wedge, 1 tablespoon whipped topping, and 1 tablespoon berries)
CALORIES 216; FAT 8.8g (sat 4.8g, mono 1.9g, poly 0.6g); PROTEIN 8g; CARB 28g; FIBER 2g; CHOL 64mg; IRON 1mg; SODIUM 308mg; CALC 125mg

TECHNIQUE TIP

Bringing the cream cheese and eggs to room temperature helps them blend more easily and makes the filling creamier and lump free.

CHOCOLATE-ALMOND CHEESECAKE BARS

Hands-on: 16 min. Total: 5 hr. 36 min.

CRUST:
⅓ cup salted dry-roasted almonds
2 tablespoons sugar
3.4 ounces all-purpose flour
  (about ¾ cup)
4 tablespoons unsalted butter,
  chilled and diced
Baking spray with flour

FILLING:
6 ounces fat-free cream cheese,
  softened
4 ounces ⅓-less-fat cream
  cheese, softened

⅔ cup sugar
½ cup plain fat-free Greek
  yogurt
1 teaspoon vanilla extract
Dash of salt
1 large egg

CHOCOLATE SWIRL:
3 ounces semisweet chocolate
  chips
1 teaspoon canola oil
2 tablespoons salted dry-roasted
  almonds, chopped

1. Preheat oven to 350°.

2. To prepare crust, place almonds and sugar in a food processor; process until finely ground. Weigh or lightly spoon flour into a dry measuring cup; level with a knife. Add flour to almond mixture; process until combined. Add butter; pulse 3 to 4 times or until mixture looks sandy. Sprinkle mixture into an 8-inch square metal baking pan coated with baking spray. Lightly press into bottom of pan. Bake at 350° for 20 minutes or until golden. Cool completely on a wire rack.

3. Reduce oven temperature to 325°.

4. To prepare filling, place cream cheeses in a medium bowl; beat with a mixer at medium speed until smooth. Add sugar, yogurt, vanilla, and salt; beat at low speed until combined. Add egg; beat 1 minute or until well combined. Pour mixture on top of cooled crust.

5. To prepare chocolate swirl, place chocolate chips and oil in a small microwave-safe bowl; microwave at HIGH 45 seconds or until chocolate melts, stirring every 15 seconds. Dollop chocolate mixture by the spoonful over cheesecake; swirl together using the tip of a knife. Sprinkle top with chopped almonds. Bake at 325° for 30 minutes or until center is almost set. Cool completely on a wire rack. Cover and chill 4 hours or overnight. Cut into 16 bars.

SERVES 16 (serving size: 1 bar)
CALORIES 175; FAT 8.9g (sat 4g, mono 3.3g, poly 0.9g); PROTEIN 5g;
CARB 20g; FIBER 1g; CHOL 26mg; IRON 1mg; SODIUM 129mg; CALC 66mg

TECHNIQUE TIP

It's easy to overbake cheesecake bars because the filling is not very thick. Be sure to check the center carefully, pulling the bars from the oven when the center still looks a little soft and wobbly.

LEMON CHEESECAKE BARS
WITH GINGERSNAP CRUST

Hands-on: 25 min. Total: 9 hr. 25 min.

CRUST:
25 gingersnap cookies
  (such as Nabisco)
2 teaspoons cornstarch
2 tablespoons butter, melted
1 teaspoon grated peeled
  fresh ginger
Baking spray with flour

FILLING:
8 ounces ⅓-less-fat cream
  cheese, softened
4 ounces fat-free cream cheese,
  softened
½ cup plus 2 tablespoons sugar

½ teaspoon vanilla extract
¼ teaspoon baking powder
⅛ teaspoon salt
2 large eggs
¼ cup light sour cream
½ teaspoon grated lemon rind
1 tablespoon fresh lemon juice

TOPPING:
⅓ cup sugar
½ teaspoon grated lemon rind
⅓ cup fresh lemon juice
2 teaspoons cornstarch
2 large egg yolks
1 teaspoon butter, softened

1. Preheat oven to 350°.

2. To prepare crust, place cookies and cornstarch in a food processor; process until finely ground. Add butter and ginger; process until moist crumbs form. Sprinkle mixture into a 9-inch square metal baking pan coated with baking spray. Lightly press into bottom of pan. Bake at 350° for 14 minutes or until toasted and fragrant. Cool completely on a rack.

3. Reduce oven temperature to 325°.

4. To prepare filling, place cream cheeses in a bowl; beat with a mixer at medium speed until smooth. Add sugar, vanilla, baking powder, and salt; beat at low speed until well combined. Add eggs, 1 at a time, beating well after each addition. Add sour cream, rind, and juice; beat until combined. Pour mixture on top of cooled crust. Bake at 325° for 30 minutes or until almost set in the middle. Remove pan from oven; place on a wire rack.

5. To prepare topping, combine sugar, rind, juice, cornstarch, and yolks in a small saucepan, stirring with a whisk until smooth. Place pan over medium-low heat; cook 5 minutes or until mixture thickens, stirring constantly. Remove pan from heat; add butter, stirring until butter melts. Spread topping over warm cheesecake. Cool completely on wire rack. Cover and refrigerate overnight. Cut into 16 bars.

SERVES 16 (serving size: 1 bar)
CALORIES 177; FAT 7.5g (sat 3.8g, mono 2.3g, poly 0.4g); PROTEIN 4g;
CARB 23g; FIBER 0g; CHOL 63mg; IRON 1mg; SODIUM 216mg; CALC 66mg

MY TOP 5 TIPS FOR
CREATING THE
BEST TEXTURE

*Making rich and creamy cheesecakes, pies, and ice creams
that are also better for you is not impossible. Through many trials
and errors, I have come up with ways to make amazing
desserts that taste like nothing is missing.*

1 *When baking eggs, milk, and cream cheese in a recipe, it is important not to overbake or bake at too high of a temperature. Both of these can lead to an off-flavored dessert that is lumpy and dry.*

2 *While fat-free cream cheese reduces saturated fat and calories, it shouldn't be used by itself when making cheesecake and cheesecake bars because it doesn't firm up when baked. Using a combination of fat-free and ⅓-less-fat cream cheeses greatly improves the texture and gives these desserts richness.*

3 *Reduced-calorie Cool Whip is my go-to ingredient for adding creaminess and volume. If you use the same amount of heavy cream, the saturated fat and calories are greatly increased— double the calories and more than triple the saturated fat. Since Cool Whip isn't something generally eaten every day, I'm OK with a modest amount of whipped topping that may include some undesirable fats.*

4 *The crystals that form in ice cream can be smooth or sharp edged, creamy or hard as concrete, and can be easily controlled by adding just a touch of corn syrup and flavored liqueurs. The corn syrup prevents sharp edges, and the alcohol controls how hard the ice cream freezes.*

5 *Using heavy cream and whole milk in moderation adds creaminess and makes textures smooth so that even just a small amount improves the recipes.*

CHERRY CHEESECAKE BROWNIES

Hands-on: 34 min. Total: 1 hr. 24 min.

½ cup chopped dried tart cherries

1 tablespoon cherry liqueur (such as kirschwasser)

1 cup sugar, divided

3 ounces ⅓-less-fat cream cheese

2 ounces fat-free cream cheese

1 tablespoon all-purpose flour

¾ teaspoon vanilla extract, divided

⅝ teaspoon baking powder, divided

Dash of salt

1 large egg, lightly beaten

Baking spray with flour

3 ounces bittersweet chocolate, finely chopped

1 ounce unsweetened chocolate, finely chopped

3 tablespoons unsalted butter, diced

2 tablespoons canola oil

2 large egg whites

1 large egg

3.9 ounces all-purpose flour (about ¾ cup)

⅛ teaspoon salt

1. Preheat oven to 325°.

2. Place cherries and liqueur in a microwave-safe bowl. Microwave at HIGH 30 seconds or until boiling; let stand 10 minutes. Place ¼ cup sugar and cream cheeses in a bowl; beat with a mixer at medium speed 1 minute or until smooth. Add flour, ¼ teaspoon vanilla, ⅛ teaspoon baking powder, salt, and egg; beat just until blended. Stir in cherry mixture.

3. Coat a 9-inch square metal baking pan with baking spray. Combine chocolates, butter, and oil in a medium microwave-safe bowl; microwave at HIGH 1 minute or until mixture melts, stirring every 20 seconds. Stir until smooth. Let stand 5 minutes. Add ½ teaspoon vanilla, egg whites, and egg, stirring with a whisk until smooth.

4. Weigh or lightly spoon flour into dry measuring cups; level with a knife. Combine flour, ¾ cup sugar, ½ teaspoon baking powder, and salt in a large bowl. Add chocolate mixture, stirring until just combined.

5. Scrape half of the brownie batter into prepared pan. Dot half of cheesecake batter on top. Top with remaining brownie batter. Dot with remaining cheesecake batter. Swirl batters using the tip of a knife. Bake at 325° for 40 minutes or until a wooden pick inserted in center comes out with moist crumbs clinging. Cool completely in pan on a wire rack. Cut into 18 bars.

SERVES 18 (serving size: 1 bar)

CALORIES 185; FAT 9.5g (sat 5.4g, mono 2g, poly 0.4g); PROTEIN 3g; CARB 23g; FIBER 1g; CHOL 38mg; IRON 1mg; SODIUM 88mg; CALC 30mg

TECHNIQUE TIP

Adding just a bit of flour and baking powder to the cheesecake batter gives it a lighter texture so that it doesn't sink underneath the brownie batter while it bakes. Cherry liqueur amps up the flavor of the cherries, but you can substitute water, if you'd prefer a non-alcoholic version.

1. Sprinkle the gelatin evenly over the water, making sure all of it touches the water.

2. If there's any unmelted chocolate after stirring it into the hot milk mixture, don't worry. It will finish melting when the gelatin dissolves.

3. When making the curls, be sure the chocolate is at room temperature. If it's too cold, it will break into shards instead of curls. Use a mix of chocolate, if you like, to make the curls.

MILK CHOCOLATE PANNA COTTA

Hands-on: 15 min. Total: 8 hr. 15 min.

Panna cotta is a naturally lighter version of crème brulée. It's a perfect dessert when you want to end a meal, particularly a heavy one, with something visually stunning that has a rich flavor. Chilling the panna cotta overnight makes the texture silky smooth.

1½ teaspoons unflavored gelatin
3 tablespoons cold water
1¾ cups 2% reduced-fat milk
2 tablespoons sugar
⅛ teaspoon salt
3 ounces milk chocolate, divided
¼ teaspoon vanilla extract

1. Sprinkle gelatin over 3 tablespoons cold water in a small bowl. Let stand 5 minutes.

2. Bring milk, sugar, and salt to a simmer in a saucepan (do not boil); remove pan from heat. Finely chop 2 ounces chocolate; add to milk mixture, stirring until chocolate melts. Return pan to low heat; add gelatin mixture. Cook 1 minute or until gelatin completely melts. Stir in vanilla. Divide mixture among 4 (6-ounce) ramekins or custard cups. Cool to room temperature. Cover and chill 8 hours or overnight.

3. To serve, run a knife around the outside edges of panna cottas. Place a plate upside down on top of each cup; invert onto plate. Using a vegetable peeler, shave 1 ounce chocolate into curls. Top panna cottas evenly with curls.

SERVES 4 (serving size: 1 panna cotta)
CALORIES 188; FAT 8.2g (sat 5.1g, mono 0.6g, poly 0.1g); PROTEIN 6g;
CARB 25g; FIBER 2g; CHOL 9mg; IRON 1mg; SODIUM 140mg; CALC 159mg

MEYER LEMON PANNA COTTA

Hands-on: 35 min. Total: 4 hr. 55 min.

This one was created with lemon fans in mind. You can substitute regular lemon juice for the Meyer lemon in a pinch. Stirring the lemon juice in at the end keeps the milk from curdling.

1 Meyer lemon
¾ cup 2% reduced-fat milk, divided
½ cup half-and-half
⅓ cup sugar
⅛ teaspoon salt
1¾ teaspoons unflavored gelatin
1½ cups low-fat buttermilk
Cooking spray
½ cup frozen reduced-calorie whipped topping (such as Cool Whip), thawed
Mint sprigs (optional)
Lemon rind strips (optional)

1. Remove rind from lemon using a vegetable peeler, avoiding the white pith. Squeeze 3 tablespoons juice from lemon. Combine rind, ½ cup milk, half-and-half, sugar, and salt in a small saucepan; bring to a simmer (do not boil). Remove pan from heat; cover and let stand 20 minutes. Discard lemon rind.

2. Sprinkle gelatin over ¼ cup milk in a small bowl; let stand 5 minutes. Return milk mixture in pan to medium heat; cook 1 minute or until mixture reaches a simmer. Whisk in gelatin mixture, stirring until gelatin completely dissolves. Stir in buttermilk and 3 tablespoons juice. Divide mixture among 4 (6-ounce) ramekins or custard cups coated with cooking spray. Cover and chill 4 hours or overnight.

3. To serve, run a knife around outside edges of panna cottas. Place a plate upside down on top of each cup; invert onto plate. Top servings with whipped topping, and garnish with mint and rind, if desired.

SERVES 4 (serving size: 1 panna cotta and 2 tablespoons whipped topping)
CALORIES 188; FAT 8.2g (sat 5.1g, mono 0.6g, poly 0.1g); PROTEIN 6g; CARB 25g; FIBER 2g; CHOL 9mg; IRON 1mg; SODIUM 140mg; CALC 159mg

MILK CHOCOLATE AND AMARETTO CRÈME BRÛLÉE

Hands-on: 30 min. Total: 5 hr. 30 min.

Milk chocolate contains more cocoa butter than dark chocolate, which means it has more saturated fat. To help balance the milk chocolate in this dessert, I added sweet, nutty Amaretto to amp up the flavor. Be sure to use high-quality milk chocolate for the best flavor and creaminess.

2 cups whole milk
¼ cup granulated sugar, divided
Dash of salt
3 ounces milk chocolate, finely chopped
2 large eggs

2 large egg yolks
1 tablespoon almond liqueur (such as Amaretto)
½ teaspoon vanilla extract
2 tablespoons superfine sugar

1. Preheat oven to 300°.

2. Bring milk, 2 tablespoons granulated sugar, and salt to a simmer in a saucepan. Remove pan from heat; add chocolate, stirring until chocolate melts. Combine 2 tablespoons granulated sugar, eggs, and egg yolks in a medium bowl; stir well with a whisk. Gradually add milk mixture to egg mixture, stirring constantly with a whisk. Stir in liqueur and vanilla.

3. Divide mixture evenly among 6 (4-ounce) ramekins or custard cups. Place cups in a 13 x 9–inch metal baking pan; add hot water to pan to a depth of 1 inch. Bake at 300° for 40 minutes or until center barely moves when dish is touched. Remove ramekins from pan; cool completely on a wire rack. Cover and chill 4 hours or overnight.

4. Sift 2 tablespoons superfine sugar evenly over custards. Holding a kitchen blowtorch about 2 inches from top of each custard, heat sugar, moving torch back and forth, until sugar is completely melted and caramelized (about 1 minute). Serve immediately.

SERVES 6 (serving size: 1 brûlée)
CALORIES 220; FAT 9.8g (sat 5.1g, mono 1.9g, poly 0.7g); PROTEIN 7g; CARB 27g; FIBER 1g; CHOL 132mg; IRON 1mg; SODIUM 96mg; CALC 129mg

1. Before sprinkling the sugar over the custards, use a paper towel to blot the tops to remove any moisture that may have accumulated. You don't want the sugar to get wet before torching it.

2. Following the manufacturer's instructions, prepare the torch. Hold the torch 2 inches (or the distance recommended by the manufacturer) above the sugar, and move it back and forth constantly to prevent one area from burning.

3. If you don't own a blowtorch, you can finish them under the broiler. Place them on a baking sheet; broil close to the heat source for 1 to 2 minutes or until the crunchy caramelized sugar crust forms.

PUMPKIN CHEESECAKE ICE CREAM

Hands-on: 18 min. Total: 4 hr. 18 min.

This flavor combination was created so that I could shoehorn ice cream into the cooler-weather months.

1½ cups whole milk
1 cup half-and-half
⅓ cup granulated sugar
⅓ cup packed brown sugar
1 teaspoon ground cinnamon
½ teaspoon ground ginger
½ teaspoon ground nutmeg

⅛ teaspoon salt
5 large egg yolks
½ cup reduced-fat sour cream
4 ounces fat-free cream cheese
¾ cup canned pumpkin puree
1 tablespoon triple sec
1 teaspoon vanilla extract

1. Combine first 8 ingredients in a large saucepan; bring to a simmer. Place egg yolks in a large bowl; stir well with a whisk. Slowly add one-third milk mixture to egg yolks, stirring constantly with a whisk. Return egg yolk mixture to milk mixture in pan. Cook over medium heat until a candy thermometer registers 160°. Immediately place pan in a large ice-filled bowl. Cool to room temperature, stirring occasionally.

2. Beat sour cream and cream cheese in a medium bowl with a mixer at medium speed until smooth; add pumpkin, beating just until combined. Stir milk mixture, triple sec, and vanilla into pumpkin mixture. Cover and chill 1 hour.

3. Pour mixture into the freezer can of a 2-quart ice-cream freezer; freeze according to manufacturer's instructions. Spoon ice cream into a freezer-safe container; cover and freeze 2 hours or until firm.

SERVES 12 (serving size: ½ cup)
CALORIES 151; FAT 6.8g (sat 3.7g, mono 2.2g, poly 0.5g); PROTEIN 5g;
CARB 17g; FIBER 1g; CHOL 92mg; IRON 0mg; SODIUM 125mg; CALC 122mg

MY TOP 5
ICE CREAM SAUCES AND TOPPINGS

Tart and bright or silky and creamy, these luscious toppings are perfect for dressing up ice cream and frozen yogurt. Easy and quick to make, the butterscotch and chocolate sauces keep well in the refrigerator for up to 2 weeks. The fruit sauces will be great for a couple of days.

1. DARK CHERRY–MERLOT SAUCE

Combine 2 cups thawed frozen pitted dark sweet cherries, 1 cup merlot wine, 2 tablespoons brown sugar, 1 teaspoon fresh lemon juice, and ⅛ teaspoon salt in a saucepan; bring to a boil. Lightly crush about half of cherries with a potato masher. Reduce heat, and cook until reduced to about 1 cup. Let stand 5 minutes.

SERVES 4 (serving size: ¼ cup)
CALORIES 120; FAT 0g (sat 0g); SODIUM 77mg

2. BUTTERSCOTCH SAUCE

Combine ½ cup brown sugar, 3 tablespoons unsalted butter, 1 tablespoon light-colored corn syrup, and ⅛ teaspoon salt in a small saucepan over medium heat; bring to a boil. Cook 3 minutes or until sugar melts and mixture is smooth; remove pan from heat. Stir in ¼ cup half-and-half and ¼ teaspoon vanilla extract (mixture will bubble). Return pan to heat; cook, without stirring, 2 minutes or until sauce is slightly thickened and bubbly. Serve warm or at room temperature.

SERVES 6 (serving size: 2 tablespoons)
CALORIES 146; FAT 6.9g (sat 4.4g); SODIUM 61mg

3. CHOCOLATE SAUCE

Combine ½ cup 2% reduced-fat milk, 3 tablespoons sugar, and 1 tablespoon unsweetened cocoa in a small saucepan, stirring with a whisk until smooth. Bring to a simmer over medium-high heat. Remove pan from heat; add ¼ cup dark chocolate chips and ¼ teaspoon vanilla extract, stirring until smooth.

SERVES 4 (serving size: about 2 tablespoons)
CALORIES 126; FAT 5.3g (sat 3.5g); SODIUM 20mg

4. MEXICAN CHOCOLATE SAUCE

Combine ½ cup 2% reduced-fat milk, 3 tablespoons sugar, 1 tablespoon unsweetened cocoa, ¼ teaspoon ground cinnamon, and dash of salt in a small saucepan, stirring with a whisk until smooth. Bring to a simmer over medium-high heat. Remove pan from heat; add ¼ cup dark chocolate chips, 1 teaspoon instant coffee, and ½ teaspoon vanilla extract, stirring until smooth.

SERVES 4 (serving size: about 2 tablespoons)
CALORIES 128; FAT 5.3g (sat 3.5g); SODIUM 56mg

5. BALSAMIC STRAWBERRIES

Combine ¼ cup packed brown sugar and 2 tablespoons balsamic vinegar in a large bowl; stir until sugar dissolves. Add 2 cups halved fresh strawberries; toss gently to coat. Let stand at room temperature 15 minutes, stirring occasionally.

SERVES 4 (serving size: ⅓ cup)
CALORIES 84; FAT 0.2g (sat 0g); SODIUM 6mg

SPICED RUM–BANANA ICE CREAM

Hands-on: 20 min. Total: 5 hr. 15 min.

Steeping whole spices in the milk mixture really gives this ice cream a wonderful combination of flavors that can still be individually identified. The riper the banana, the deeper the banana flavor will be.

2 cups whole milk
1 cup half-and-half
¾ cup packed brown sugar
1 teaspoon grated peeled fresh ginger
½ teaspoon ground nutmeg
½ teaspoon whole cloves
¼ teaspoon salt
½ vanilla bean, split
1 (3-inch) cinnamon stick
1 star anise
5 large egg yolks
1 cup mashed ripe banana
1 tablespoon spiced rum

1. Combine first 10 ingredients in a medium saucepan; bring to a simmer. Remove pan from heat; cover and let stand 20 minutes.

2. Strain mixture through a sieve into a bowl; discard solids. Return mixture to pan; bring to a simmer. Place egg yolks in a large bowl; stir well with a whisk. Slowly add milk mixture to eggs, stirring constantly with a whisk. Return mixture to pan. Cook over medium heat until a candy thermometer registers 160° (about 5 minutes). Immediately place pan in a large ice-filled bowl. Cool to room temperature, stirring occasionally. Stir in banana and rum. Cover and chill 1 hour.

3. Pour mixture into the freezer can of an ice-cream freezer; freeze according to manufacturer's instructions. Spoon ice cream into a freezer-safe container; cover and freeze 2 hours or until firm.

SERVES 12 (serving size: ½ cup)
CALORIES 147; FAT 5.6g (sat 2.9g, mono 1.2g, poly 0.4g); PROTEIN 3g;
CARB 21g; FIBER 1g; CHOL 88mg; IRON 2mg; SODIUM 82mg; CALC 90mg

RUM

Spiced rum is heavy with clove, cinnamon, and vanilla—just a little adds so much flavor. If you have only clear or gold rum, it's fine to substitute. Just a little bit of alcohol keeps the ice cream's texture creamy, but you can leave out the alcohol if you prefer.

BROWN SUGAR ICE CREAM
WITH CINNAMON GRAPE-NUTS

Hands-on: 25 min. Total: 4 hr. 40 min.

Stirring Grape-Nuts cereal into vanilla ice cream is a New England thing. I like the idea of tiny, crunchy bits in my ice cream, but not if they taste wheaty. So to kick up this Yankee-inspired dessert, I candied the cereal with a little bit of butter, sugar, and cinnamon.

2 cups whole milk
1 cup half-and-half
½ cup packed dark brown sugar
2 tablespoons dark corn syrup
Dash of salt
5 large egg yolks
3 tablespoons granulated sugar, divided
1 tablespoon brandy
2 teaspoons vanilla extract
1 tablespoon unsalted butter
½ cup Grape-Nuts cereal
½ teaspoon ground cinnamon

1. Combine first 5 ingredients in a saucepan; bring to a simmer. Combine yolks and 2 tablespoons granulated sugar in a large bowl, stirring with a whisk. Gradually add hot milk mixture to egg mixture, stirring constantly with a whisk. Return mixture to pan; cook over medium heat until a candy thermometer registers 160°, stirring constantly. Immediately place pan in an ice-filled bowl. Cool to room temperature, stirring occasionally. Stir in brandy and vanilla. Cover and chill 1 hour.

2. Melt butter in a small skillet over medium heat. Add cereal, 1 tablespoon granulated sugar, and cinnamon; cook 1 minute, stirring constantly. Cool completely.

3. Pour ice-cream mixture into the freezer can of an ice-cream freezer; freeze according to manufacturer's instructions. Spoon ice cream into a freezer-safe container. Stir in two-thirds of candied Grape-Nuts. Cover and freeze 2 hours or until firm. Sprinkle servings with remaining cereal.

SERVES 10 (serving size: ½ cup ice cream and about 1 teaspoon candied cereal)
CALORIES 187; FAT 7.9g (sat 4.2g, mono 2.5g, poly 0.7g); PROTEIN 4g; CARB 25g; FIBER 1g; CHOL 109mg; IRON 3mg; SODIUM 85mg; CALC 96mg

TECHNIQUE TIP

The cereal can quickly become overbrowned and taste burned, so keep the cook time at 1 minute; be sure to stir and check it constantly.

CHERRY GELATO

Hands-on: 19 min. Total: 3 hr. 59 min.

Gelato gets its thick creamy texture from an abundance of egg yolks. But to help limit the amount of saturated fat, I used fewer egg yolks and added cornstarch to help thicken the custard base. Make sure you let your ice-cream maker run the full time to get that dense, creamy texture that makes gelato so magical.

1½ cups whole milk
1 cup half-and-half
¾ cup sugar, divided
Dash of salt
2½ tablespoons cornstarch
5 large egg yolks

12 ounces fresh ripe cherries, pitted
1 tablespoon cherry liqueur (such as kirschwasser)
2 teaspoons fresh lemon juice
1 teaspoon vanilla extract

1. Bring milk, half-and-half, ¼ cup sugar, and salt to a simmer in a medium saucepan (do not boil). Whisk together ¼ cup sugar, cornstarch, and egg yolks in a medium bowl until smooth. Slowly pour hot milk mixture into egg mixture, stirring constantly. Return egg mixture to pan. Cook over medium heat 2 minutes or until thick and bubbly. Immediately place pan in an ice-filled bowl. Cool to room temperature, stirring occasionally.

2. Place cherries, ¼ cup sugar, liqueur, juice, and vanilla in a food processor; pulse 5 to 6 times or until finely chopped. Stir cherry mixture into cooled custard. Cover with plastic wrap, pressing onto surface of mixture. Chill 1 hour.

3. Pour cherry mixture into the freezer can of an ice-cream freezer; freeze according to manufacturer's instructions. Spoon gelato into a freezer-safe container; cover and freeze 2 hours or until firm.

SERVES 10 (serving size: ½ cup)
CALORIES 174; FAT 6.3g (sat 3.2g, mono 2.1g, poly 0.6g); PROTEIN 4g; CARB 26g; FIBER 1g; CHOL 105mg; IRON 0mg; SODIUM 45mg; CALC 82mg

TECHNIQUE TIP

Using fresh ripe cherries is the key to great cherry flavor in this gelato. If fresh cherries aren't available, use frozen dark sweet cherries that are thawed.

STRAWBERRY FROZEN YOGURT

Hands-on: 15 min. Total: 3 hr. 15 min.

I wanted this frozen yogurt to be creamy with a tart finish, so full-fat Greek yogurt was a natural. Adding a touch of whole milk made the consistency just right for the ice-cream freezer to work well, and a tiny bit of alcohol keeps the texture from getting rock hard.

1 pound fresh strawberries, chopped (about 3 cups)
2/3 cup sugar
1/4 cup light-colored corn syrup
1 tablespoon vodka

2 teaspoons fresh lemon juice
1 1/2 cups plain 10% fat Greek yogurt
1/4 cup whole milk

1. Place first 5 ingredients in a food processor; process until smooth. Strain strawberry mixture through a sieve over a large bowl; discard solids. Add yogurt and milk; stir with a whisk until well combined.

2. Pour mixture into the freezer can of an ice-cream freezer; freeze according to manufacturer's instructions. Scrape mixture into a freezer-safe container; cover and freeze 2 hours or until firm.

SERVES 8 (serving size: 1/2 cup)
CALORIES 179; FAT 4.8g (sat 3.5g, mono 0.1g, poly 0.1g); PROTEIN 3g; CARB 31g; FIBER 1g; CHOL 8mg; IRON 0mg; SODIUM 23mg; CALC 57mg

Be patient and only make this sherbet in the summer when the cantaloupes are at their absolute ripest. The wait will be worth it, I promise. Here's some science behind that statement: Many fruits are harvested when their sugar content has reached a certain level, like grapes for making wine. Just out of curiosity, *Cooking Light* tested the sugar level of a cantaloupe in January when it was out of season and discovered that a melon picked during peak season (June through August) had more than 50% more sugar.

CANTALOUPE SHERBET

Hands-on: 25 min. Total: 3 hr.

This creamy sherbet captures the absolute essence of the melon, delivering a refreshing summertime dessert. It may seem like overkill adding light corn syrup to a frozen dessert, but corn syrup helps create smaller ice crystals, resulting in a smoother, creamier texture.

¾ cup water
½ cup sugar
¼ cup light-colored corn syrup
⅛ teaspoon salt
4 cups chopped cantaloupe
   (about a 3-pound melon)

2 tablespoons vodka (optional)
1 tablespoon fresh lime juice
2 tablespoons heavy cream

1. Bring first 4 ingredients to a boil in a saucepan; cook 1 minute or until sugar dissolves. Remove pan from heat. Place pan in a large ice-filled bowl for 15 minutes or until sugar mixture cools completely, stirring occasionally.

2. Place cantaloupe, vodka, if desired, and juice in a food processor; process until smooth. Strain cantaloupe mixture through a sieve over a bowl; discard solids. Add sugar mixture and cream to cantaloupe mixture; stir well.

3. Pour cantaloupe mixture into the freezer can of an ice-cream freezer; freeze according to manufacturer's instructions. Spoon sherbet into a freezer-safe container; cover and freeze 2 hours or until firm.

SERVES 10 (serving size: about ½ cup)
CALORIES 96; FAT 1.3g (sat 0.7g, mono 0.3g, poly 0.1g); PROTEIN 1g;
CARB 22g; FIBER 1g; CHOL 4mg; IRON 0mg; SODIUM 46mg; CALC 9mg

CRANBERRY MOJITO GRANITA

Hands-on: 7 min. Total: 3 hr. 27 min.

Granita is the perfect icy treat to showcase a fun summery alcoholic beverage. Fresh mint and freshly squeezed lime juice really perk up this chilly dessert. When making the sugar syrup, make sure all the sugar has dissolved before removing the pan from the heat. Adding the mint to the sugar syrup after it has been taken off the heat keeps the mint from becoming bitter and infusing the syrup with an unpleasant flavor.

1 cup water
½ cup sugar
¼ cup light-colored corn syrup
Dash of salt
⅓ cup packed mint leaves

1 cup cranberry juice cocktail
½ cup rum (light or gold)
3 tablespoons fresh lime juice
Grated lime rind (optional)

1. Bring first 4 ingredients to a boil in a saucepan. Remove pan from heat. Add mint; cover and let stand 20 minutes. Discard mint.

2. Combine sugar mixture and cranberry juice, rum, and lime juice in an 8-inch square freezer-safe dish. Freeze 1 hour. Stir mixture with a fork, scraping sides. Repeat process every 45 minutes until completely frozen and scraped. Garnish with lime rind, if desired.

SERVES 6 (serving size: about ½ cup)
CALORIES 176; FAT 0.1g (sat 0g, mono 0g, poly 0.1g); PROTEIN 0g; CARB 35g; FIBER 0g; CHOL 0mg; IRON 1mg; SODIUM 36mg; CALC 15mg

1. Scraping every 45 minutes instead of after the granita is a solid block creates smaller ice crystals and makes it melt-in-your-mouth smooth instead of hard and icy. Otherwise, it's really nothing more than a snow cone! This is what it looks like after 1 hour in the freezer.

2. 45 minutes later.

3. And then 45 minutes after that.

4. Finished and perfectly fluffy.

BLOOD ORANGE AND PROSECCO GRANITA

Hands-on: 6 min. Total: 3 hr. 36 min.

Scraping every 45 minutes is the key to this dessert. When you follow this procedure, the payoff is beyond compare. The granita will last longer in the freezer, staying separated and snowy until it's gone. The distinctive ruby-fleshed blood orange can vary in flavor from tart citrus to sweet like a tangerine. You can substitute other sweet wines like cava, Gewürztraminer, or sweet ice wine for the prosecco.

1 cup cold water
½ cup sugar
1 tablespoon light-colored corn syrup

Dash of salt
1½ cups cold blood orange juice
1 cup cold prosecco or cava

1. Combine first 4 ingredients in a bowl; stir with a whisk until sugar dissolves. Stir in juice and wine. Pour mixture into an 8-inch square freezer-safe dish. Freeze 1 hour. Stir with a fork, scraping sides. Repeat process every 45 minutes until completely frozen and scraped.

SERVES 6 (serving size: ½ cup)
CALORIES 144; FAT 0g; PROTEIN 0g; CARB 30g; FIBER 0g; CHOL 0mg; IRON 0mg; SODIUM 27mg; CALC 1mg

BLOOD ORANGES

Blood oranges—the primary orange grown in Italy—owe their unique reddish flesh to the very cool nights of the areas where they're grown. They taste like a combination of orange and pine with spicy flavor notes.

LABORS
OF LOVE

COCONUT CAKE
WITH RASPBERRY FILLING AND ITALIAN MERINGUE ICING

Hands-on: 35 min. Total: 2 hr. 10 min.

My Aunt Wanda was a wonderful cake maker. She would make a version of this cake for my birthday every year, with the lightest, fluffiest, creamiest Italian meringue. Omit the liqueur if you prefer; just add a little water in its place to make the filling spreadable.

FILLING:
2 pints fresh raspberries (12 ounces)
⅓ cup sugar
2 tablespoons water
⅛ teaspoon salt
3 tablespoons cornstarch
3 tablespoons Chambord (raspberry-flavored liqueur)

CAKE:
Baking spray with flour
8 ounces cake flour (about 2 cups)
2 ounces coconut flour (about ½ cup), lightly toasted
2 teaspoons baking powder
½ teaspoon salt
1½ cups sugar, divided
⅓ cup canola oil
2 tablespoons butter, softened
1 teaspoon vanilla extract
1 cup coconut water
6 large egg whites

ICING:
3 large egg whites
¼ teaspoon cream of tartar
½ cup sugar
3 tablespoons water
⅛ teaspoon salt
½ cup unsweetened coconut flakes, toasted

1. To prepare filling, combine first 4 ingredients in a saucepan; bring to a boil. Cook over medium heat 5 minutes or until berries soften and begin to fall apart. Combine cornstarch and liqueur in a small bowl, stirring with a whisk until smooth. Add cornstarch mixture to raspberry mixture, stirring with a whisk; return to a boil. Cook 1 minute or until very thick, stirring constantly. Spoon mixture into a bowl; cover and refrigerate until needed.

2. Preheat oven to 350°. Coat 3 (8-inch) cake pans with baking spray; line bottom of pans with wax paper. Coat wax paper with baking spray.

3. To prepare cake, weigh or lightly spoon flours into dry measuring cups; level with a knife. Combine flours, baking powder, and salt in a bowl; stir with a whisk. Place 1¼ cups sugar, oil, butter, and vanilla in a large bowl. Beat with a mixer at medium speed 5 minutes or until fluffy. Add coconut water; beat at low speed 1 minute or until combined. Add flour mixture; beat at low speed 1 minute or until well combined.

4. Beat 6 egg whites with a mixer at high speed until medium peaks form using clean, dry beaters. Add ¼ cup sugar, 1 tablespoon at a time.

Stir one-fourth of egg white mixture into batter; gently fold in remaining egg whites. Divide batter evenly among prepared pans. Bake at 350° for 19 minutes or until a wooden pick inserted in center comes out clean. Cool in pans 10 minutes on a wire rack. Remove from pans; cool completely on wire rack. Discard wax paper.

5. To prepare icing, place 3 egg whites and cream of tartar in a large bowl; beat with a mixer at medium speed 2 minutes or until foamy. Increase mixer speed to high; beat 2 to 3 minutes or until soft peaks form. Combine ½ cup sugar, 3 tablespoons water, and ⅛ teaspoon salt in a saucepan; bring to a boil. Cook, without stirring, until a candy thermometer registers 230°. With mixer on low speed, pour hot sugar syrup in a thin stream down the side of mixing bowl. Gradually increase speed to high; beat 3 minutes or until thick and cool.

6. To assemble cake, place 1 cake layer on a serving plate; spread with one-half of filling, leaving a ½-inch border. Top with another cake layer. Spread with remaining filling, leaving a ½-inch border. Top with remaining cake layer. Spread icing over top and sides of cake. Gently press toasted coconut into sides of cake.

SERVES 16 (serving size: 1 slice)
CALORIES 294; FAT 8.7g (sat 3.4g, mono 3.4g, poly 1.5g); PROTEIN 4g;
CARB 49g; FIBER 3g; CHOL 4mg; IRON 1mg; SODIUM 225mg; CALC 45mg

TRIPLE CHOCOLATE LAYER CAKE

Hands-on: 25 min. Total: 2 hr. 45 min.

Even your most demanding chocoholic will be satisfied with this trio: deep chocolate cake layers with a creamy milk chocolate filling topped with bittersweet chocolate glaze.

CAKE:

1 cup boiling water
½ cup plus 1 tablespoon unsweetened cocoa
2 ounces bittersweet chocolate, finely chopped
Baking spray with flour
1½ cups granulated sugar
¼ cup unsalted butter, softened
3 tablespoons canola oil
1 teaspoon vanilla extract
3 large egg whites
10 ounces cake flour (about 2½ cups)
1½ teaspoons baking powder
½ teaspoon baking soda
¼ teaspoon salt

FILLING:

⅓ cup 2% reduced-fat milk
1 tablespoon granulated sugar
1 tablespoon cornstarch
Dash of salt
3.5 ounces milk chocolate, finely chopped
¾ cup frozen reduced-calorie whipped topping (such as Cool Whip), thawed

GLAZE:

½ cup powdered sugar
¼ cup unsweetened cocoa
1 ounce bittersweet chocolate, finely chopped
3 tablespoons 2% reduced-fat milk
1 tablespoon light-colored corn syrup

1. Preheat oven to 350°.

2. To prepare cake, combine boiling water and ½ cup cocoa. Add bittersweet chocolate; stir until smooth. Cool to room temperature (about 10 minutes). Coat 2 (8-inch) round metal cake pans with baking spray; line bottoms of pans with wax paper. Coat wax paper with baking spray; dust pans with remaining 1 tablespoon cocoa.

3. Place 1½ cups granulated sugar, butter, canola oil, and vanilla in a large bowl; beat with a mixer at medium speed until well combined, about 2 minutes. Add egg whites, 1 at a time, beating well after each addition. Weigh or lightly spoon flour into dry measuring cups; level with a knife. Combine flour, baking powder, baking soda, and salt in a bowl, stirring with a whisk. Alternately add flour mixture and cocoa mixture to butter mixture, beginning and ending with flour mixture; beat until just combined.

4. Divide batter evenly between prepared pans. Bake at 350° for 26 minutes or until a wooden pick inserted in center comes out with moist crumbs clinging. Cool in pans 15 minutes on wire racks. Remove from pans; cool completely on wire racks. Discard wax paper.

5. To prepare filling, combine milk, sugar, cornstarch, and salt in a saucepan; bring to a boil, stirring constantly. Cook 1 minute or until very thick, stirring constantly. Remove pan from heat. Add milk chocolate; stir until chocolate melts and mixture is smooth. Scrape mixture into a bowl; cover and chill completely. Uncover and fold in whipped topping. Cover and chill 30 minutes.

6. To prepare glaze, combine powdered sugar and remaining ingredients in a saucepan over low heat. Cook 1 minute or until chocolate melts, stirring frequently. Place 1 cake layer on a plate. Spread filling over cake, leaving a ¼-inch border. Top with remaining layer, pressing lightly. Drizzle warm glaze over top and down sides of cake.

SERVES 16 (serving size: 1 slice)
CALORIES 292; FAT 10.1g (sat 5.3g, mono 2.7g, poly 1g); PROTEIN 4g; CARB 50g; FIBER 2g; CHOL 8mg; IRON 2mg; SODIUM 160mg; CALC 56mg

MY TOP 5
BEYOND-THE-BASICS TOOLS

There are so many specialized (and expensive) tools for the kitchen, some useful, and some ridiculous (the RoboStir comes to mind). But, if you are an avid or wannabe avid dessert-maker, here is a list of extras that are wonderful and worthwhile to have on hand.

1 *Light-colored metal 9-inch springform pan. You can use a springform pan for so many baked goods: cheesecakes, single-layer tall cakes, chilled layer cakes, ice cream cakes— the opportunities are endless.*

2 *Light-colored metal 9-inch removable-bottom tart pan. If you enjoy tarts, whether sweet or savory, a tart pan with a removable bottom is essential to an accurately baked crust and a beautiful presentation.*

3 *A couple of high-quality thermometers. These are critical to some high-heat methods. First, a sturdy glass candy thermometer with a durable clip that attaches to the sides of a pan makes it easy to monitor sugary syrups hands free. Second, an instant-read probe thermometer tells you immediately that the recipe is at the target temperature.*

4 *Light-colored metal heavy jelly-roll pans. They are perfect not only for baking extremely thin cake layers, but for toasting nuts, coconut, and even spices. I prefer to use a light-colored metal pan so I can more easily see the amount of browning. A dark pan makes this more difficult.*

5 *Heavy-duty kitchen torch. If you love crème brûlée and caramelized meringues, upgrade your tiny hand-held torch to a Bernzomatic torch. Try making rainy-day indoor s'mores with it!*

BAKED CHOCOLATE MOUSSE

Hands-on: 20 min. Total: 8 hr. 52 min.

Light, silky, and rich with three types of chocolate, this baked mousse is like eating a chocolate cloud. Be sure to whip the egg mixture for the full 5 minutes to get the best texture in the finished mousse.

½ cup water
⅓ cup Dutch process cocoa
1 teaspoon instant espresso
4 ounces bittersweet chocolate, finely chopped
1 ounce unsweetened chocolate, finely chopped
1 tablespoon brandy
½ teaspoon vanilla extract
2 large eggs
2 large egg whites
⅓ cup sugar
Dash of salt
2 cups frozen reduced-calorie whipped topping, thawed and divided
Baking spray with flour
½ cup fresh raspberries

1. Preheat oven to 350°.

2. Bring ½ cup water to a boil in a small saucepan. Add cocoa and espresso, stirring until smooth. Remove pan from heat. Add chocolates, stirring gently until chocolates melt and mixture is smooth. Stir in brandy and vanilla. Pour chocolate mixture into a large bowl. Let stand 10 minutes, stirring occasionally.

3. Combine eggs, egg whites, sugar, and salt in the top of a double boiler. Cook over simmering water until sugar melts and a thermometer registers 120° (about 2 minutes), stirring constantly with a whisk. Pour egg mixture into a medium bowl; beat with a mixer at high speed until thick and ribbony, about 5 minutes.

4. Stir one-third of egg mixture into chocolate mixture; gently fold in remaining egg mixture. Gently fold 1½ cups whipped topping into chocolate mixture. Spoon batter into an 8-inch springform pan coated with baking spray. Smooth top.

5. Bake at 350° for 25 minutes or until almost set. Cool completely in pan on a wire rack. Cover and chill overnight (or at least 4 hours). To serve, run a knife around edge of pan; remove sides of pan. Top servings with a dollop of whipped topping and raspberries.

SERVES 10 (serving size: 1 wedge, about 1 tablespoon whipped topping, and about 1 tablespoon raspberries)
CALORIES 166; FAT 9.6g (sat 5.4g, mono 1g, poly 0.3g); PROTEIN 4g; CARB 19g; FIBER 2g; CHOL 38mg; IRON 2mg; SODIUM 51mg; CALC 21mg

TECHNIQUE TIP

Folding frozen whipped topping that's been thawed into mousse, and then baking it was a first for me. The fact that the whipped topping was also reduced calorie resulted in a significant "aha" moment in the Test Kitchen when the finished chocolate mousse cake was perfectly creamy, dense, and absolutely delicious. Be very gentle when folding the ingredients together. Stop folding when the white streaks are gone, and not one more second.

EXTREME LEMON AND CHOCOLATE ROULADE

Hands-on: 45 min. Total: 3 hr. 15 min.

Lemon and chocolate are a lovely and lively pair in this rolled cake. If you prefer milder lemon flavor, omit the rind from the filling. Or, if you are a bold lemon-lover (like me), don't strain the rind out of the filling—enjoy the tartness and texture it provides.

CAKE:

Baking spray with flour
3 ounces cake flour
   (about ¾ cup)
⅓ cup unsweetened cocoa, sifted
1 teaspoon baking powder
⅛ teaspoon salt
5 large eggs, separated
¾ cup granulated sugar,
   divided
1 teaspoon vanilla extract
¼ teaspoon cream of tartar
2 tablespoons powdered sugar

FILLING:

⅔ cup granulated sugar, divided
1 tablespoon grated lemon rind
6 tablespoons fresh lemon juice
3 tablespoons unsalted butter,
   divided
⅛ teaspoon salt
1 tablespoon cornstarch
3 large egg yolks
2 large eggs
1½ cups frozen reduced-calorie
   whipped topping, thawed
1 tablespoon powdered sugar

1. Preheat oven to 350°. Lightly coat a jelly-roll pan with baking spray. Line bottom of pan with wax paper. Coat paper with baking spray. Set aside.

2. To prepare cake, weigh or lightly spoon flour into a dry measuring cup; level with a knife. Combine flour, cocoa, baking powder, and salt in a bowl; stir with a whisk. Place egg yolks, ¼ cup sugar, and vanilla in a large bowl; beat with a mixer at medium speed until light and fluffy, about 4 minutes. Place egg whites and cream of tartar in a medium bowl; beat at medium speed until foamy using clean, dry beaters. Beat mixture at high speed until soft peaks form. Gradually add ½ cup sugar, 1 tablespoon at a time, beating until stiff peaks form (do not overbeat). Stir one-fourth of egg white mixture into egg yolk mixture; gently fold in remaining egg white mixture. Sift one-half of flour mixture over top of egg mixture; gently fold in. Sift remaining flour mixture over top of egg mixture; gently fold in. Spread mixture evenly into prepared pan.

3. Bake at 350° for 9 minutes or until cake springs back when lightly touched in the center. Loosen cake from sides of pan; turn out onto a dish towel dusted with 2 tablespoons powdered sugar. Carefully peel off wax paper; cool 1 minute. Starting at narrow end, roll up the cake and towel together. Place, seam side down, on a wire rack; cool completely (about 1 hour).

4. To prepare filling, place ⅓ cup sugar, rind, juice, 2 tablespoons butter, and salt in a small saucepan over medium heat. Cook until butter and sugar melt, stirring frequently (about 4 minutes). Place ⅓ cup sugar, cornstarch, egg yolks, and eggs in a bowl; stir well with a whisk until smooth. Drizzle hot juice mixture into egg mixture, stirring constantly with a whisk. Return mixture to pan. Cook over medium heat until mixture thickens and a candy thermometer registers 180° (do not boil). Pour mixture through a sieve into a small bowl, pressing on solids. Discard solids. Add 1 tablespoon butter, stirring until butter melts and is combined. Cover surface of mixture with plastic wrap. Chill completely.

5. To assemble roulade, gently stir whipped topping into chilled lemon filling. Unroll cake carefully; remove towel. Spread lemon filling over cake, leaving a 1-inch border around outside edges. Reroll cake; place, seam side down, on a platter. Cover and chill 1 hour. Sprinkle cake with 1 tablespoon powdered sugar. Cut cake into slices.

SERVES 10 (serving size: 1 slice)
CALORIES 285; FAT 9.8g (sat 5.2g, mono 2.9g, poly 1.1g); PROTEIN 7g;
CARB 45g; FIBER 1g; CHOL 195mg; IRON 2mg; SODIUM 161mg; CALC 61mg

PECAN STICKY WEDGES

Hands-on: 58 min. Total: 11 hr.

These heavenly yeast wedges develop even more flavor when the prepared dough is refrigerated overnight. Just let them sit at room temperature for 30 minutes, and then pop them in the oven for about 30 minutes. Inspired by Joy of Cooking's he-man-sized buns that have 629 calories and 14 grams of saturated fat each, this recipe yields gooey, sticky slices containing a third of the calories and saturated fat.

1 package dry yeast
   (about 2¼ teaspoons)
¼ cup warm water (100° to 110°)
⅓ cup granulated sugar
¼ cup 2% reduced-fat milk
1 teaspoon vanilla extract
1 teaspoon salt
2 large eggs
12.4 ounces all-purpose flour
   (about 2¾ cups), divided

9 tablespoons unsalted butter,
   softened and divided
Cooking spray
1 cup packed dark brown sugar,
   divided
3 tablespoons light-colored corn
   syrup
2 tablespoons mild honey
⅔ cup chopped pecans
2 teaspoons ground cinnamon

1. Combine yeast and warm water in the bowl of a stand mixer or a large bowl; stir with a whisk. Let stand 5 minutes or until foamy. Add granulated sugar, milk, vanilla, salt, and eggs; beat at low speed until well combined (about 1 minute).

2. Weigh or lightly spoon flour into dry measuring cups; level with a knife. Add ¼ cup flour to yeast mixture; beat at low speed 1 minute or until well combined. Add 2¼ cups flour; beat at low speed until combined and a soft dough forms. Change paddle to dough hook; beat 8 minutes on medium speed or until smooth and elastic, scraping bottom and sides of bowl occasionally. Add 5 tablespoons butter, 1 tablespoon at a time, beating at low speed until combined after each addition and scraping sides, if necessary. Scrape dough onto a work surface sprinkled with ¼ cup flour (dough will be sticky). Knead dough 1 minute or until smooth and elastic. Place dough into a large bowl coated with cooking spray. Cover and place in a warm place (85°), free from drafts, 1 hour or until doubled in bulk.

3. Combine 3 tablespoons butter, ⅔ cup brown sugar, corn syrup, and honey in a small saucepan; bring to a boil, stirring just until butter melts. Boil 30 seconds, stirring constantly. Pour syrup into a 12-cup Bundt pan coated with cooking spray. Sprinkle nuts over syrup. Cool completely.

4. Combine ⅓ cup brown sugar and cinnamon in a small bowl, stirring with a whisk.

5. Turn dough out onto a lightly floured surface. Gently press dough into a 16 x 12–inch rectangle. Melt 1 tablespoon butter. Brush surface of dough with melted butter. Sprinkle brown sugar–cinnamon mixture evenly over dough. Beginning at short side, roll up dough jelly-roll fashion; pinch seam to seal. Carefully lift roll, and fit into prepared pan. Pinch ends together. Cover with plastic wrap, and chill overnight.

6. Preheat oven to 350°.

7. Remove pan from refrigerator. Let stand at room temperature 30 minutes. Bake at 350° for 28 to 30 minutes or until a wooden pick inserted in center comes out clean and dry. Cool in pan 4 minutes on a wire rack. Place a plate upside down on top of pan; invert onto plate. Cool slightly before cutting.

SERVES 16 (serving size: 1 wedge)

CALORIES 265; FAT 10.8g (sat 4.7g, mono 3.9g, poly 1.5g); PROTEIN 4g; CARB 40g; FIBER 1g; CHOL 41mg; IRON 1mg; SODIUM 160mg; CALC 21mg

ROASTED GRAPE AND PEAR KUCHEN

Hands-on: 27 min. Total: 3 hr.

½ cup warm 2% reduced-fat milk
(100° to 110°)
1 package dry yeast
(about 2¼ teaspoons)
½ cup granulated sugar, divided
2 tablespoons canola oil, divided
1 teaspoon vanilla extract
1 teaspoon grated lemon rind
½ teaspoon salt
½ teaspoon ground nutmeg
2 large eggs
9 ounces all-purpose flour
(about 2 cups)

6 tablespoons unsalted butter,
softened and divided
Baking spray with flour
1½ cups seedless red grapes
2 firm peeled pears, cut into
¼-inch-thick slices
¼ cup chopped pecans
3 tablespoons brown sugar
½ teaspoon ground cinnamon
1½ cups frozen reduced-calorie
whipped topping (such as
Cool Whip), thawed

1. Combine milk, yeast, and ½ teaspoon sugar in a large bowl, stirring with a whisk. Let stand 5 minutes or until mixture bubbles.

2. Add remaining granulated sugar, 1 tablespoon oil, vanilla, rind, salt, nutmeg, and eggs; beat with a mixer at low speed until well combined. Weigh or lightly spoon flour into dry measuring cups; level with a knife. Add flour; beat at low speed 5 minutes or until batter is smooth. Add 5 tablespoons butter, 1 tablespoon at a time, beating until fully combined after each addition. Smooth batter evenly into a 9-inch springform pan coated with baking spray. Cover and let rise in a warm place (85°), free from drafts, 1½ hours.

3. Preheat oven to 450°.

4. Combine 1 tablespoon oil, grapes, and pears; arrange mixture in a single layer on a baking sheet. Bake at 450° for 20 to 25 minutes or until tender and beginning to caramelize. Cool completely. Reduce oven temperature to 350°.

5. Melt 1 tablespoon butter. Combine grape mixture, melted butter, pecans, brown sugar, and cinnamon in a bowl; toss gently to coat. Arrange mixture on top of dough. Bake at 350° for 30 minutes or until a wooden pick inserted in center comes out dry. Cool in pan 15 minutes on a wire rack. Remove from pan; place on a platter. Serve wedges with a dollop of whipped topping.

SERVES 12 (serving size: 1 wedge and 2 tablespoons whipped topping)
CALORIES 281; FAT 12.4g (sat 5.5g, mono 4.4g, poly 1.7g); PROTEIN 5g;
CARB 39g; FIBER 2g; CHOL 47mg; IRON 1mg; SODIUM 124mg; CALC 39mg

TECHNIQUE TIP

For best flavor, use instant yeast, not rapid-rise. Letting the yeast do its thing for the full 1½ hours develops amazing flavor. When roasting the pears and grapes, let the fruit cook until it gets completely soft and develops a beautiful browned, caramelized exterior. Caramelizing the fruit ahead removes excess moisture that would make the cake soggy, so let the oven work its magic and don't be tempted to skimp on the roasting time.

ALMOND AND CITRUS STOLLEN

Hands-on: 35 min. Total: 3 hr.

When I was in the Baking and Pastry Arts program at the Culinary Institute of America, my bread class chef-instructor made the most delicious Stollen bread I had ever tasted. While his was rich with butter, almond paste, candied fruit, and nuts, this lightened version is my homage to Chef Kastel's artistry in the oven. Wrap the second loaf well, and it will keep up to 2 weeks.

SPONGE:
4.8 ounces bread flour
   (about 1 cup)
3 teaspoons dry yeast
1 teaspoon sugar
½ cup warm 2% reduced-fat milk
   (100° to 110°)

FINAL DOUGH:
¼ cup sugar
1 ounce almond paste, crumbled
1 tablespoon grated orange rind
1 tablespoon grated lemon rind
1 teaspoon vanilla extract
10 tablespoons unsalted butter,
   softened
7.2 ounces bread flour
   (about 1½ cups)

1 teaspoon salt
⅓ cup packed golden raisins
⅓ cup packed raisins
3 tablespoons fresh orange juice

FILLING:
3 tablespoons sugar
1 tablespoon unsalted butter,
   softened
2 ounces almond paste, crumbled
1½ cups sliced almonds,
   divided

FINISH:
1 tablespoon unsalted butter,
   melted
2 tablespoons sugar

1. To prepare sponge, weigh or lightly spoon flour into a dry measuring cup; level with a knife. Combine flour, yeast, sugar, and warm milk; stir well (mixture is stiff). Cover and let rise in a warm place (85°), free from drafts, 30 minutes.

2. To prepare dough, beat sugar and almond paste at medium speed in a stand mixer with paddle attachment until mixture looks sandy, about 1 minute. Add rinds, vanilla, and butter; beat 1 minute or until combined (do not overbeat). Add sponge; beat 1 minute at low speed or until combined. Change mixer paddle to dough hook. Weigh or lightly spoon bread flour into dry measuring cups; level with a knife. Add flour and salt to sponge mixture; beat at low speed with dough hook 6 to 8 minutes or until smooth and elastic. Remove bowl from mixer; cover with plastic wrap, and let rise in a warm place (85°), free from drafts, 30 minutes.

3. While dough rises, combine raisins and juice in a microwave-safe bowl. Microwave at HIGH 20 seconds. Cover bowl with plastic wrap; let stand 20 minutes.

4. To prepare filling, combine sugar, butter, and almond paste in a bowl; beat with a mixer at low speed until completely combined (mixture will be crumbly). Add ½ cup almonds; beat at low speed 30 seconds or until well combined.

5. Return dough bowl to mixer. Add raisin mixture and 1 cup almonds; beat at low speed with dough hook 2 minutes or until well combined. Scrape dough out onto a lightly floured surface. Divide dough into 2 equal pieces. Press each piece into a 9- to 10-inch circle. Arrange half of filling on one-half of the dough circle. Fold over dough and pinch edges to seal. Repeat process with remaining dough and filling. Place loaves on doubled baking sheets covered with parchment paper. Cover lightly with plastic wrap, and let stand in a warm place (85°), free from drafts, 30 minutes.

6. Preheat oven to 350°. Remove plastic wrap from loaves. Bake at 350° for 35 to 40 minutes or until golden, rotating pan after 20 minutes. Remove pan from oven. To finish loaves, brush top and sides with melted butter. Cool completely on a wire rack. Sprinkle top, bottom, and sides of loaves with sugar.

SERVES 20 (serving size: 1 slice)
CALORIES 228; FAT 12g (sat 4.9g, mono 4.8g, poly 1.5g); PROTEIN 5g;
CARB 27g; FIBER 2g; CHOL 19mg; IRON 1mg; SODIUM 122mg; CALC 42mg

LEMON AND ALMOND SOUFFLÉS

Hands-on: 16 min. Total: 36 min.

I love a restaurant that offers a soufflé that you must order at the same time you order your entrée. The anticipation of the warm, creamy, cloudlike perfection makes me rush through dinner. For these lovely lemony soufflés, you can prepare the ramekins and the egg yolk mixture ahead, and then whip the egg white mixture at the last minute, fold them together, and pop them in the oven. They're easy and very impressive. Take care when beating the egg whites; overbeating them will make the soufflés fall before they are fully cooked. Dust the tops lightly with powdered sugar just before serving, if you like.

Cooking spray
½ cup plus 2 tablespoons sugar, divided
2 large egg yolks
1.1 ounces all-purpose flour (about ¼ cup)
¾ cup low-fat buttermilk
1 tablespoon grated lemon rind
⅓ cup fresh lemon juice
2 tablespoons butter, melted
6 large egg whites, at room temperature
¼ teaspoon cream of tartar
¼ cup sliced almonds

1. Place a baking sheet in oven. Preheat oven to 425°.

2. Lightly coat 6 (8-ounce) ramekins with cooking spray; sprinkle with 2 tablespoons sugar, tilting dishes to coat sides completely.

3. Combine ¼ cup sugar and egg yolks in a large bowl; beat with a mixer at high speed until thick and pale (about 2 minutes). Weigh or lightly spoon flour into a dry measuring cup; level with a knife. Add flour, buttermilk, and next 3 ingredients (through butter); beat at medium speed 1 minute or until completely combined.

4. Combine egg whites and cream of tartar in a large bowl; beat at medium speed until foamy using clean, dry beaters. Beat at high speed until soft peaks form. Reduce speed to medium, and add ¼ cup sugar, 1 tablespoon at a time. Beat at high speed until medium peaks form (do not overbeat). Gently stir one-fourth of egg whites into lemon mixture; gently fold in remaining egg whites. Divide mixture among prepared ramekins. Sprinkle tops with almonds. Remove baking sheet from oven; place dishes on preheated baking sheet. Return baking sheet to oven. Immediately reduce oven temperature to 350°; bake at 350° for 20 minutes or until puffy and lightly browned. Serve immediately.

SERVES 6 (serving size: 1 soufflé)
CALORIES 213; FAT 8g (sat 3.5g, mono 3.1g, poly 0.9g); PROTEIN 7g;
CARB 29g; FIBER 1g; CHOL 74mg; IRON 1mg; SODIUM 91mg; CALC 68mg

1. Lightly spray the ramekins with cooking spray; you don't want a puddle collecting in the bottoms. Add the sugar, and tilt the ramekins so every inch is coated with sugar; dump the excess sugar into the next ramekin and repeat.

2. Beating the egg whites to medium peaks gives them room to stretch in the oven, and not break and deflate the soufflé before it's served.

3. Stirring some of the egg whites into the soufflé base starts lightening up the batter so that the remaining whites can be folded in easily. Clean off any spills from the top edge of the ramekins to prevent the soufflé from sticking and not rising all the way.

MY TOP 5 TIPS FOR
CONTROLLING
TEMPERATURE

*Since so many of the recipes in this chapter have
temperature-sensitive instructions, here are
my top tips on how to manage the highs and the lows.*

1 *Unless specifically called for (like chilled butter in pie dough),
ingredients should be at room temperature. So what is room
temperature? In a bakeshop, room temperature is between 65° and
70°. If butter is too warm, it will not hold air whipped into it during
the creaming process that makes cake layers rise, or it will melt too
quickly, making cookies spread farther than intended. If flour is
too cold, it will take cakes and breads longer to bake, resulting in
dry loaves and layers. If eggs are too cold when added to butter
and sugar mixtures, the butter will get chilled and form little lumps,
resulting in holes in the cake layers. The easiest way to avoid trouble
with temperature is to read the recipe all the way through and make
sure all your ingredients are at the temperature recommended.*

2 *When making bread or other baked goods with yeast, the ideal
rising temperature is 80° to 85°. If the recipe calls for a second
rise or resting the dough on the counter, room temperature (65° to
70°) will be fine. If you have a proof mode on your oven, use it.*

3 *Some of the fillings and batters are chilled in the refrigerator
and may be pretty thick or stiff when removed. Before you
lighten them with whipped topping or meringue, stir the chilled
filling with a whisk to make it creamy again. The fillings will be
much easier to fold together afterwards.*

4 *I know, you're anxious to dig into the cheesecake or panna
cotta, but really, allowing them to chill overnight or for
the minimum number of hours recommended will absolutely make
a noticeable difference in the texture and even in the flavors.
Be patient; you'll be glad you were.*

5 *Use your thermometers. The difference between soft ball and
hard ball stages is only about 10°, but the difference in results
is light years apart. A crisp candy garnish or brittle will be a sticky
pulling mess if the temperature of the sugar syrup is not accurate.*

ORANGE MARMALADE NOCKERL

Hands-on: 25 min. Total: 39 min.

If you love soufflé, you are going to be nuts about Nockerl, a beautifully light yet creamy soufflé originating in Austria. When it is served in Salzburg, the meringue is shaped like the nearby rugged snowcapped mountain range.

¼ cup half-and-half
2 tablespoons orange marmalade
½ teaspoon vanilla extract
Baking spray with flour
6 tablespoons granulated sugar, divided
4 large egg yolks
⅛ teaspoon salt
2 tablespoons cake flour
2 teaspoons grated orange rind
7 large egg whites
¼ teaspoon cream of tartar
2 tablespoons powdered sugar

1. Preheat oven to 400°.

2. Combine half-and-half, marmalade, and vanilla in the bottom of an 1½-quart glass or ceramic baking dish coated with baking spray, stirring with a whisk.

3. Place 3 tablespoons sugar, yolks, and salt in a medium bowl, and beat with a mixer at medium-high speed until light and fluffy, about 3 minutes. Add flour and rind; beat 30 seconds or until well combined. Place yolk mixture in a large bowl. Beat egg whites and cream of tartar at medium speed until foamy using clean, dry beaters. Add 3 tablespoons granulated sugar, 1 tablespoon at a time, beating at high speed until stiff peaks form (do not overbeat). Stir one-third of egg white mixture into egg yolk mixture. Gently fold in remaining egg white mixture. Scoop mixture into prepared dish (do not smooth top). Place on bottom rack in oven. Bake at 400° for 14 minutes or until golden. Sprinkle top with powdered sugar. Serve immediately.

SERVES 8 (serving size: 1 cup)
CALORIES 118; FAT 3.2g (sat 1.4g, mono 1g, poly 0.4g); PROTEIN 5g; CARB 17g; FIBER 0g; CHOL 95mg; IRON 0mg; SODIUM 95mg; CALC 24mg

PUMPKIN-HAZELNUT LAYERED CHEESECAKE

Hands-on: 1 hr. Total: 13 hr.

Using low-fat and fat-free cream cheeses to lighten a cheesecake isn't new, but adding a little flour and baking powder helps lighten their texture, making it creamy and smooth. Toasting the hazelnut meal really boosts its flavor in the cake layer. Instead of buying hazelnut meal, you can toast whole nuts, let them cool completely, and process in a food processor until finely ground. If you prefer, you can skip brushing the cake with the Frangelico liqueur.

CAKE:

2.25 ounces hazelnut meal
  (about ½ cup)
½ cup sugar
2 tablespoons unsalted butter,
  softened
2 tablespoons canola oil
2 large egg whites (reserve yolks
  for cheesecake)
1.5 ounces all-purpose flour
  (about ⅓ cup)
2 teaspoons cornstarch
½ teaspoon baking powder
¼ teaspoon salt
Baking spray with flour
1 tablespoon hazelnut-flavored
  liqueur (such as Frangelico)

CHEESECAKE:

12 ounces ⅓-less-fat cream
  cheese
4 ounces fat-free cream cheese
¾ cup sugar
3 large eggs
2 large egg yolks
  (reserved from cake)
2 tablespoons all-purpose flour
1 teaspoon vanilla extract
1 teaspoon ground cinnamon
½ teaspoon ground ginger
½ teaspoon ground allspice
½ teaspoon baking powder
¼ teaspoon salt
¼ teaspoon ground cloves
1 cup canned pumpkin puree

BRITTLE:

⅓ cup sugar
1 tablespoon water
3 tablespoons hazelnuts, roasted
  and coarsely chopped
Cooking spray
1 cup frozen fat-free whipped
  topping, thawed

1. Preheat oven to 350°.

2. To prepare cake, sprinkle hazelnut meal evenly on a rimmed baking sheet. Bake at 350° for 4 to 5 minutes or until lightly browned, stirring after 3 minutes. Cool completely (about 20 minutes).

3. Combine sugar, butter, and oil in a large bowl; beat with a mixer at medium speed until well combined, about 3 minutes. Add egg whites; beat 1 minute. Weigh or lightly spoon flour into a dry measuring cup;

level with a knife. Combine flour, toasted hazelnut meal, cornstarch, baking powder, and salt in a bowl; stir with a whisk. Add flour mixture to sugar mixture; beat at low speed 1 minute or until just combined. Spoon batter into a 9-inch springform pan coated with baking spray; smooth top. Bake at 350° for 13 minutes or until a wooden pick inserted in center comes out clean. Brush top of hot cake with hazelnut liqueur. Cool completely in pan on a wire rack (do not remove or loosen sides of springform pan). Reduce oven temperature to 325°.

4. While cake cools, prepare cheesecake: Place cream cheeses in a large bowl; beat at medium speed 2 minutes or until smooth. Add sugar and next 10 ingredients (through cloves); beat at low speed 2 minutes or until well combined. Add pumpkin; beat at low speed until combined. Pour cheesecake batter over top of cooled hazelnut cake. Bake at 325° for 50 minutes or until cheesecake center barely moves when pan is touched. Remove cheesecake from oven. Run a knife around outside edge. Cool completely on a wire rack. Cover and chill 8 hours or overnight.

5. To prepare brittle, place sugar and 1 tablespoon water in a small heavy saucepan over medium heat; cook until sugar dissolves, stirring occasionally. Continue cooking about 2 minutes or until golden (do not stir). While sugar mixture cooks, sprinkle chopped hazelnuts over a 14 x 2–inch area on parchment paper lightly coated with cooking spray. Drizzle caramelized sugar over nuts. Cool 10 minutes or until firm; break into 14 pieces. To serve, cut cheesecake into wedges, dollop each wedge with whipped topping, and top with brittle.

SERVES 14 (serving size: 1 cheesecake wedge, about 1 tablespoon whipped topping, and 1 piece brittle)
CALORIES 292; FAT 14.9g (sat 5.2g, mono 6.7g, poly 1.8g); PROTEIN 7g; CARB 33g; FIBER 2g; CHOL 90mg; IRON 1mg; SODIUM 276mg; CALC 96mg

TROPICAL PAVLOVAS

Hands-on: 52 min. Total: 6 hr. 52 min.

1. Use a dark color pen or pencil to draw 4-inch circles on the parchment paper so that when the paper in turned upside down the marks will still be visible.

2. Adding lots of sugar to this meringue makes it creamier and thicker so that it holds its shape in the oven and develops a crisp texture. Add the sugar slowly so that it gets fully incorporated and inhibits the whites from whipping up stiffly.

3. Scoop the meringue into a mound in the center of each circle. Using a spoon, shape each meringue into a nest, building the sides up and carving out the centers.

4 large eggs, separated and divided
¼ teaspoon cream of tartar
⅛ teaspoon salt, divided
⅔ cup sugar
¼ teaspoon vanilla extract
½ cup dry-roasted, salted macadamia nuts, finely chopped and divided
¾ cup unsweetened pineapple juice
¼ cup sugar, divided
2 teaspoons fresh lime juice
1 tablespoon cornstarch
1 large egg
1 tablespoon unsalted butter
½ cup diced pineapple
½ cup diced mango
½ cup diced kiwi (about 2)
½ cup small fresh raspberries
1 tablespoon thinly sliced fresh mint
1 tablespoon fresh lime juice
½ cup unsweetened coconut flakes, toasted

1. Preheat oven to 250°. Draw 8 (4-inch) circles on parchment paper. Turn parchment paper over; secure paper to a large baking sheet with masking tape.

2. Beat egg whites, cream of tartar, and a dash of salt with a mixer at medium speed until foamy (about 1 minute). Increase speed to high; beat until soft peaks form (about 1 minute). With mixer at medium speed add sugar, 1 tablespoon at a time, beating well after each addition. Beat at high speed until stiff peaks form (do not overbeat). Beat in vanilla. Reserve 3 tablespoons chopped nuts. Gently fold remaining nuts into egg mixture. Divide egg white mixture among the 8 drawn circles. Shape meringues into nests with 1-inch sides using the back of a spoon. Sprinkle reserved 3 tablespoon nuts over tops of meringue nests. Bake at 250° for 2 hours or until dry, rotating pan after 1 hour. Turn oven off; cool meringues in closed oven at least 4 hours. Carefully remove meringues from paper. Store in an airtight container until ready to use.

3. Combine pineapple juice, 2 tablespoons sugar, lime juice, and a dash of salt in a saucepan; bring to a simmer. Combine 2 tablespoons sugar, cornstarch, egg, and egg yolks in a bowl, stirring with a whisk until smooth. Gradually drizzle juice mixture into egg mixture, stirring constantly with a whisk. Return mixture to pan. Cook over medium heat until mixture thickens and a candy thermometer registers 180°. Remove pan from heat; stir in butter. Place pan in a large ice-filled bowl; bring curd to room temperature, stirring occasionally.

4. Combine pineapple and next 5 ingredients in a bowl; toss gently.

5. To assemble pavlovas, top each meringue with about 2 tablespoons curd, ¼ cup fruit relish, and 1 tablespoon toasted coconut. Serve immediately.

SERVES 8 (serving size: 1 pavlova)
CALORIES 269; FAT 13g (sat 5.4g, mono 6.2g, poly 0.6g); PROTEIN 5g;
CARB 36g; FIBER 3g; CHOL 73mg; IRON 1mg; SODIUM 137mg; CALC 32mg

TORCHED ALASKA

Hands-on: 1 hr. 20 min. Total: 5 hr. 30 min.

Using Swiss meringue and scorching it with a kitchen torch yields yummy caramelized bits and eliminates the tricky baking part of a traditional baked Alaska—the potential melted mess. Chocolate and coffee ice creams create a mocha treat, but you can use any ice cream combination you prefer.

CAKE:
Baking spray with flour
2.7 ounces cake flour
 (about ⅔ cup)
¾ teaspoon baking powder
¼ teaspoon salt
4 large eggs, separated
⅓ cup sugar, divided
1½ teaspoons vanilla extract
¼ teaspoon cream of tartar

FILLING:
1½ cups reduced-fat coffee
 ice cream
1½ cups fat-free chocolate
 ice cream

MERINGUE:
5 large egg whites
⅓ cup sugar
¼ teaspoon vanilla extract
¼ teaspoon cream of tartar
Dash of salt

1. Preheat oven to 400°. Lightly coat a jelly-roll pan with baking spray. Line bottom of pan with wax paper; coat paper with baking spray.

2. To prepare cake, weigh or lightly spoon flour into dry measuring cups; level with a knife. Combine flour, baking powder, and salt, stirring with a whisk.

3. Place egg yolks and 2 tablespoons sugar in a large bowl; beat with a mixer at medium speed until thick and ribbony, about 4 minutes. Beat in vanilla.

4. Place egg whites and cream of tartar in a large bowl; using clean dry beaters, beat at medium speed until foamy (about 30 seconds). Increase speed to high, and beat until medium peaks form. Add remaining sugar, 1 tablespoon at a time, beating until stiff peaks form (about 2 minutes). Stir one-fourth of egg whites into egg yolk mixture. Gently fold remaining whites into yolk mixture. Sift one-half of flour mixture over top of egg mixture; gently fold in. Sift remaining half of flour mixture over batter; gently fold in. Scrape batter into prepared pan; spread evenly in pan with an offset spatula.

5. Bake at 400° for 9 minutes or until lightly browned and cake springs back when lightly touched. Run a knife around outside edge; cool in pan 4 minutes. Turn pan upside down onto a wire rack; remove cake. Carefully remove wax paper; discard paper. Cool cake completely on wire rack. Using a 3½-inch round cookie cutter, cut 12 circles from cake. Discard remaining cake scraps.

6. To prepare filling, lightly coat 6 (8-ounce) ramekins with baking spray. Line each ramekin with plastic wrap, allowing the plastic wrap to extend over edges. Spoon ¼ cup coffee ice cream into bottom of each ramekin, spreading evenly; top each with 1 cake round. Spread ¼ cup chocolate ice cream over each cake layer, spreading evenly; top each with 1 cake round. Cover with plastic wrap; freeze 4 hours or up to overnight.

7. To prepare meringue, combine 5 egg whites and remaining ingredients in the top of a double boiler. Cook over simmering water 2 to 3 minutes or until a candy thermometer registers 160°, stirring constantly with a whisk. Remove from heat. Beat egg mixture with a mixer at medium speed until soft peaks form (about 6 minutes); beat at high speed until stiff peaks form.

8. Invert ramekins, cake sides down, onto a baking sheet; discard plastic wrap. Divide meringue evenly among servings, and spread evenly over each dome (the domes should be completely covered with meringue). Holding a kitchen torch about 3 inches from domes, heat the meringue, moving the torch back and forth until lightly browned. Transfer to individual plates, and serve immediately.

SERVES 6 (serving size: 1 Torched Alaska)
CALORIES 250; FAT 4g (sat 1.7g, mono 0.8g, poly 0.5g); PROTEIN 9g; CARB 45g; FIBER 2g; CHOL 93mg; IRON 1mg; SODIUM 255mg; CALC 118mg

PINEAPPLE SHORTBREAD CAKES

Hands-on: 1 hr. 13 min. Total: 2 hr. 18 min.

3 (8-ounce) cans crushed
   pineapple in juice, undrained
¾ cup granulated sugar
½ teaspoon salt, divided
⅓ cup light-colored corn syrup
4 teaspoons all-purpose flour
9 ounces cake flour (about
   2¼ cups)

⅓ cup nonfat dry milk
¼ teaspoon baking powder
12 tablespoons unsalted butter,
   softened
½ cup plus 1 tablespoon
   powdered sugar, divided
2 large egg yolks

1. Drain pineapple in a fine-mesh sieve, pressing on solids; discard or save juice for another use. Place pineapple in a medium saucepan over medium-low heat; cook 15 minutes or until all the liquid has evaporated, stirring frequently. Add sugar and ¼ teaspoon salt; cook 8 to 10 minutes or until liquid is absorbed and mixture thickens, stirring frequently. Add corn syrup; cook 5 minutes or until mixture is very thick and sticky, stirring frequently. Add all-purpose flour; cook 1 minute or until mixture is very thick, stirring constantly. Scrape mixture onto a baking sheet, and spread into a thin layer; cover and chill completely (about 20 minutes).

2. Weigh or lightly spoon cake flour into dry measuring cups; level with a knife. Place flour, dry milk, ¼ teaspoon salt, and baking powder in a fine-mesh sieve. Place butter in a large bowl; beat with a mixer at medium speed until smooth and creamy. Add ½ cup powdered sugar, and beat 2 minutes or until well combined. Add egg yolks, 1 at a time, beating well after each addition. Beat 2 minutes or until fluffy. Add flour mixture; beat at low speed until just combined. Divide dough in half. Shape into 2 (10-inch) logs; cover each with plastic wrap, and chill 30 minutes.

3. Preheat oven to 325°.

4. Cut each log into 12 equal pieces. Working with 1 piece at a time, roll dough into a 3-inch circle on a lightly floured surface. Place about 1 tablespoon filling in the center; bring edges together, and pinch closed. Gently press into a floured 1¾-inch square mold (cookie cutter) or shape into a square by hand. Repeat procedure with remaining dough and filling; place cake 2 inches apart on parchment-lined baking sheets. Bake at 325° for 25 minutes, turning cake over and rotating pans after 15 minutes. Remove cake from pans, and cool completely on wire racks. Sprinkle with 1 tablespoon powdered sugar.

SERVES 24 (serving size: 1 cake)
CALORIES 168; FAT 6.3g (sat 3.8g, mono 1.7g, poly 0.3g); PROTEIN 2g;
CARB 27g; FIBER 0g; CHOL 31mg; IRON 1mg; SODIUM 68mg; CALC 34mg

DRY MILK

Why add dry milk to these shortbread cakes? It provides structure and strength to baked goods and enhances browning, all without adding additional liquid to the recipe. It's important to push the dry milk through a fine-mesh sieve because it tends to clump in hard granules; they need to be broken up for these cakes to have the right texture. Many large bakeries use dry milk in their cakes, muffins, and breads because it takes up less space, is more economical than liquid milk, and still provides flavor and quality to their products.

RASPBERRY SPICE BUNS

Hands-on: 45 min. Total: 3 hr. 1 min.

1 package dry yeast
  (about 2¼ teaspoons)
⅔ cup warm 2% reduced-fat
  milk (100° to 110°)
½ cup sugar
7 tablespoons unsalted butter,
  softened and divided
5.6 ounces all-purpose flour
  (about 1¼ cups)
5.2 ounces einkorn flour
  (about 1¼ cups)

1 large egg
1 teaspoon ground cinnamon
¾ teaspoon salt
½ teaspoon ground allspice
¼ cup all-purpose flour for
  kneading and shaping
Cooking spray
¼ cup raspberry jam

1. Stir yeast into warm milk; let stand 5 minutes or until foamy.

2. Combine sugar and 6 tablespoons butter in a large bowl of a stand mixer; beat 1 minute or until combined (do not overbeat). Weigh or lightly spoon flours into dry measuring cups; level with a knife. Place flours in a bowl, stirring with a whisk. Add ½ cup flour mixture, yeast mixture, and egg to butter mixture; beat at low speed 2 minutes or until well combined. Beat in cinnamon, salt, and allspice. Add remaining flour mixture to butter mixture; beat at low speed with dough hook 8 minutes or until smooth and elastic, stopping to scrape sides and bottom of bowl 2 times. Scrape dough out onto a floured work surface; knead 1 minute, using as little additional all-purpose flour as possible to keep from sticking to surface. Place dough in a large bowl coated with cooking spray. Cover and let rise in a warm place (85°), free from drafts, 1½ hours.

3. Turn dough out onto a lightly floured surface. Divide dough into 12 equal pieces. Lightly press each piece into a 3-inch circle. Drop 1 teaspoon jam into center of each circle. Gather edges together, and pinch to seal. Place sealed edge in bottom of muffin cups coated with cooking spray. Lightly cover pan with plastic wrap. Place in a warm place (85°), free from drafts, 30 minutes.

4. Preheat oven to 350°.

5. Remove plastic wrap from dough. Bake at 350° for 14 to 15 minutes or until lightly browned, rotating pan after 7 minutes. Cool in pan 2 minutes; remove from pan, and place on a wire rack. Melt 1 tablespoon butter. Brush tops of buns with butter. Serve warm or at room temperature.

SERVES 12 (serving size: 1 bun)

CALORIES 215; FAT 8g (sat 4.6g, mono 2.1g, poly 0.5g); PROTEIN 4g;
CARB 32g; FIBER 1g; CHOL 34mg; IRON 1mg; SODIUM 159mg; CALC 26mg

TECHNIQUE TIP

Use as little flour on your work surface as possible when kneading and shaping these little buns. If you use too much, the dough will look gray instead of light brown. Substitute your favorite jam if you are not a fan of raspberry. Apple butter would go wonderfully well with the cinnamon and allspice added to the dough.

SMOKED CHERRY BOMBS

Hands-on: 45 min. Total: 1 hr. 12 min.

At less than 100 calories, these little bombs pack a great cherry and almond blast. Use red dye-free cherries made with pure cane sugar for the best real cherry flavor.

½ cup cherrywood smoking chips
12 maraschino cherries with
    stems (such as Tillen Farms)
2 ounces almond paste
5 teaspoons sugar, divided
2 ounces ⅓-less-fat cream
    cheese, softened

¼ teaspoon vanilla extract
Dash of salt
4 (14 x 9–inch) sheets frozen
    phyllo dough, thawed
3 tablespoons butter, melted

1. Preheat oven to 375°.

2. Pierce 10 holes on one side of the bottom of a 13 x 9–inch disposable aluminum foil pan. Place holes over element on cooktop; place smoking chips over holes inside pan. Heat element under holes to medium-high; let burn 1 minute or until chips begin to smoke. Arrange cherries on opposite end of pan. Carefully cover pan with foil. Reduce heat to low; smoke cherries 5 minutes. Smoking the cherries for 5 minutes may not seem like very much time, but it's the perfect amount of time to create a blend of smoky and sweet. Do not open the foil top during this 5 minutes or the balance goes out of whack. Seriously. Remove from heat; let stand until cool.

3. Place almond paste and 1 tablespoon sugar in a bowl; beat with a mixer at medium speed until mixture looks sandy. Add cream cheese, vanilla, and salt; beat 1 minute or until well combined.

4. Place 1 phyllo sheet on a large cutting board or work surface (cover remaining dough to keep from drying); lightly brush with melted butter. Sprinkle with ½ teaspoon sugar. Repeat layers with remaining phyllo, butter (saving a little butter for the outsides), and sugar. Cut 12 (3.5 x 3–inch) rectangles through phyllo layers using a pizza cutter or a sharp knife. Spoon about 1 teaspoon almond mixture into center of each phyllo stack. Press 1 cherry, stem up, into almond mixture. Gather edges of phyllo, and press around stem to seal, forming a pouch. Gently brush outsides with remaining butter. Place on a baking sheet covered with parchment paper. Bake at 375° for 12 to 13 minutes or until crisp. Remove bombs from baking sheet, and place on a wire rack. Cool completely.

SERVES 12 (serving size: 1 cherry bomb)
CALORIES 87; FAT 5.5g (sat 2.6g, mono 2g, poly 0.5g); PROTEIN 1g; CARB 8g;
FIBER 0g; CHOL 11mg; IRON 0mg; SODIUM 70mg; CALC 15mg

SMOKING CHERRIES

1. Pierce one end of the aluminum foil pan with the tip of a knife 10 to 15 times to allow the heat to easily penetrate the pan.

2. Place the wood chips over the holes in the pan, and then place the pan over the flame or heating element. The wood chips will begin smoking; if they flame up, reduce the heat.

3. Arrange the cherries on the opposite end of the pan; cover the pan with foil to hold in the smoke. The aluminum pan gets very hot, so use thick potholders or a dry kitchen towel to protect your hands from burns.

Temperature control is the key to creating marshmallows with great texture. Cooking the syrup to 250° will give the marshmallows a fluffy yet firm texture and prevent the gelatin from taking over and turning them into gummy bears. Letting the sugar syrup cool to 210° gives it the right viscosity to start whipping and incorporating air right away. If your sugar syrup gets too cool, it will stick to the bowl and the beaters and you won't be able to whip it to incorporate air. If you start whipping too soon, it will just take a lot longer to get the ultimate marshmallow texture you want.

CHOCOLATE MARSHMALLOWS

Hands-on: 50 min. Total: 2 hr. 50 min.

As is so true with many homemade goodies, once you experience an honest-to-goodness homemade marshmallow, store-bought will never pass your lips again.

1 cup water, divided
3 (¼-ounce) packages
   unflavored gelatin
1½ cups granulated sugar
1 cup light-colored corn syrup
Dash of salt
1 teaspoon vanilla extract

¼ cup sifted unsweetened cocoa
Cooking spray
⅓ cup powdered sugar
⅓ cup cornstarch
2 teaspoons unsweetened cocoa
2 ounces bittersweet chocolate,
   finely chopped

1. Pour ½ cup water into a microwave-safe bowl; sprinkle gelatin on top.

2. Combine ½ cup water, sugar, corn syrup, and salt in a medium, heavy saucepan over medium-high heat; bring to a boil, stirring frequently. Cook, without stirring, until a candy thermometer registers 250°. Pour sugar mixture into the bowl of a stand mixer; let stand until thermometer registers 210° (about 15 minutes).

3. Microwave gelatin mixture at HIGH 20 seconds or until gelatin melts, stirring after 10 seconds. With mixer at low speed, beat sugar mixture using whip attachment; gradually pour gelatin mixture in a thin stream into sugar mixture. Beat in vanilla. Increase speed to high; whip mixture until light and fluffy (about 5 minutes). Reduce mixer to low speed, and gradually add ¼ cup cocoa; beat until well combined. Using a spatula coated with cooking spray, scrape mixture into an 11 x 7–inch glass or ceramic baking dish coated with cooking spray; smooth top. Let stand at room temperature 2 hours.

4. Sift together powdered sugar, cornstarch, and 2 teaspoons cocoa into a jelly-roll pan. Using an offset spatula coated with cooking spray, remove marshmallow from pan; place in powdered sugar mixture. Using scissors well coated with powdered sugar mixture, cut marshmallows into 78 (1-inch) squares. Dust marshmallows with powdered sugar mixture; shake to remove excess mixture.

5. Arrange marshmallows on a wire rack placed on parchment paper. Place bittersweet chocolate in a small microwave-safe bowl; microwave at HIGH 30 seconds or until chocolate melts, stirring after 15 seconds. Drizzle chocolate over marshmallows; let stand until chocolate sets.

SERVES 26 (serving size: 3 marshmallows)
CALORIES 113; FAT 1.2g (sat 0.6g, mono 0.1g, poly 0g); PROTEIN 1g; CARB 27g;
FIBER 0g; CHOL 0mg; IRON 0mg; SODIUM 16mg; CALC 4mg

NUTRITIONAL INFORMATION

How to Use It and Why

Glance at the end of any *Cooking Light* recipe, and you'll see how committed we are to helping you make the best of today's light cooking. With chefs, registered dietitians, home economists, and a computer system that analyzes every ingredient we use, *Cooking Light* gives you authoritative dietary detail like no other magazine. We go to such lengths so you can see how our recipes fit into your healthful eating plan. If you're trying to lose weight, the calorie and fat figures will probably help most. But if you're keeping a close eye on the sodium, cholesterol, and saturated fat in your diet, we provide those numbers, too. And because many women don't get enough iron or calcium, we can help there, as well. Finally, there's a fiber analysis for those of us who don't get enough roughage.

Here's a helpful guide to put our nutritional analysis numbers into perspective. Remember, one size doesn't fit all, so take your lifestyle, age, and circumstances into consideration when determining your nutrition needs. For example, pregnant or breast-feeding women need more protein, calories, and calcium. And women older than 50 need 1,200mg of calcium daily, 200mg more than the amount recommended for younger women.

In Our Nutritional Analysis, We Use These Abbreviations

sat	saturated fat	CARB	carbohydrates	g	gram
mono	monounsaturated fat	CHOL	cholesterol	mg	milligram
poly	polyunsaturated fat	CALC	calcium		

Daily Nutrition Guide

	Women ages 25 to 50	Women over 50	Men ages 24 to 50	Men over 50
Calories	2,000	2,000 or less	2,700	2,500
Protein	50g	50g or less	63g	60g
Fat	65g or less	65g or less	88g or less	83g or less
Saturated Fat	20g or less	20g or less	27g or less	25g or less
Carbohydrates	304g	304g	410g	375g
Fiber	25g to 35g	25g to 35g	25g to 35g	25g to 35g
Cholesterol	300mg or less	300mg or less	300mg or less	300mg or less
Iron	18mg	8mg	8mg	8mg
Sodium	2,300mg or less	1,500mg or less	2,300mg or less	1,500mg or less
Calcium	1,000mg	1,200mg	1,000mg	1,000mg

The nutritional values used in our calculations either come from The Food Processor, Version 10.4 (ESHA Research), or are provided by food manufacturers.

METRIC EQUIVALENTS

The information in the following charts is provided to help cooks outside the United States successfully use the recipes in this book. All equivalents are approximate.

Cooking/Oven Temperatures

	Fahrenheit	Celsius	Gas Mark
Freeze Water	32° F	0° C	
Room Temp.	68° F	20° C	
Boil Water	212° F	100° C	
Bake	325° F	160° C	3
	350° F	180° C	4
	375° F	190° C	5
	400° F	200° C	6
	425° F	220° C	7
	450° F	230° C	8
Broil			Grill

Liquid Ingredients by Volume

¼ tsp	=					1 ml		
½ tsp	=					2 ml		
1 tsp	=					5 ml		
3 tsp	=	1 Tbsp	=	½ fl oz	=	15 ml		
2 Tbsp	=	⅛ cup	=	1 fl oz	=	30 ml		
4 Tbsp	=	¼ cup	=	2 fl oz	=	60 ml		
5⅓ Tbsp	=	⅓ cup	=	3 fl oz	=	80 ml		
8 Tbsp	=	½ cup	=	4 fl oz	=	120 ml		
10⅔ Tbsp	=	⅔ cup	=	5 fl oz	=	160 ml		
12 Tbsp	=	¾ cup	=	6 fl oz	=	180 ml		
16 Tbsp	=	1 cup	=	8 fl oz	=	240 ml		
1 pt	=	2 cups	=	16 fl oz	=	480 ml		
1 qt	=	4 cups	=	32 fl oz	=	960 ml		
				33 fl oz	=	1000 ml	=	1 l

Dry Ingredients by Weight

(To convert ounces to grams, multiply the number of ounces by 30.)

1 oz	=	¹⁄₁₆ lb	=	30 g
4 oz	=	¼ lb	=	120 g
8 oz	=	½ lb	=	240 g
12 oz	=	¾ lb	=	360 g
16 oz	=	1 lb	=	480 g

Length

(To convert inches to centimeters, multiply the number of inches by 2.5.)

1 in	=					2.5 cm		
6 in	=	½ ft			=	15 cm		
12 in	=	1 ft			=	30 cm		
36 in	=	3 ft	=	1 yd	=	90 cm		
40 in	=					100 cm	=	1 m

Equivalents for Different Types of Ingredients

Standard Cup	Fine Powder (ex. flour)	Grain (ex. rice)	Granular (ex. sugar)	Liquid Solids (ex. butter)	Liquid (ex. milk)
1	140 g	150 g	190 g	200 g	240 ml
¾	105 g	113 g	143 g	150 g	180 ml
⅔	93 g	100 g	125 g	133 g	160 ml
½	70 g	75 g	95 g	100 g	120 ml
⅓	47 g	50 g	63 g	67 g	80 ml
¼	35 g	38 g	48 g	50 g	60 ml
⅛	18 g	19 g	24 g	25 g	30 ml

INDEX

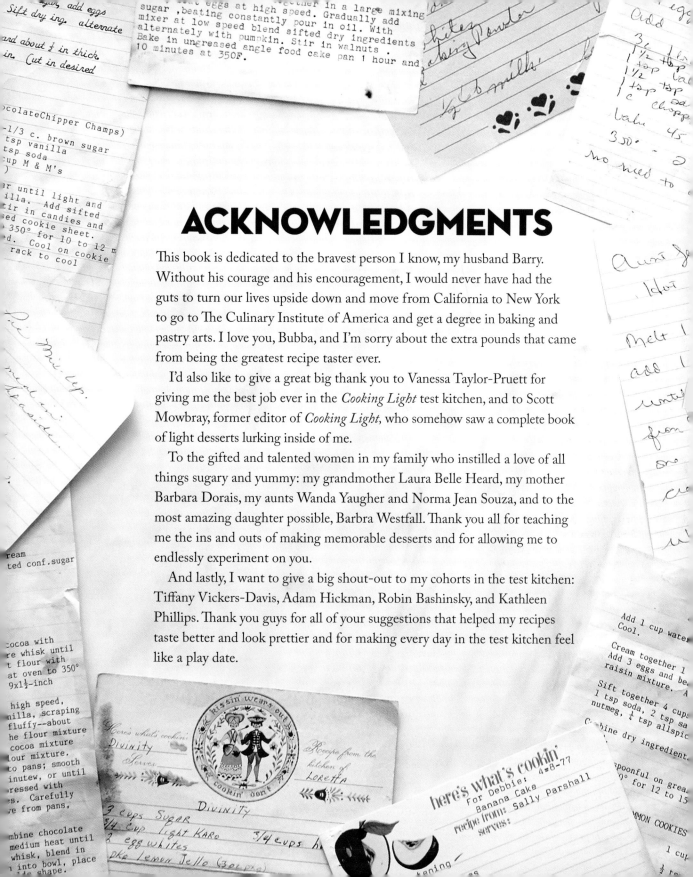

ACKNOWLEDGMENTS

This book is dedicated to the bravest person I know, my husband Barry. Without his courage and his encouragement, I would never have had the guts to turn our lives upside down and move from California to New York to go to The Culinary Institute of America and get a degree in baking and pastry arts. I love you, Bubba, and I'm sorry about the extra pounds that came from being the greatest recipe taster ever.

I'd also like to give a great big thank you to Vanessa Taylor-Pruett for giving me the best job ever in the *Cooking Light* test kitchen, and to Scott Mowbray, former editor of *Cooking Light*, who somehow saw a complete book of light desserts lurking inside of me.

To the gifted and talented women in my family who instilled a love of all things sugary and yummy: my grandmother Laura Belle Heard, my mother Barbara Dorais, my aunts Wanda Yaugher and Norma Jean Souza, and to the most amazing daughter possible, Barbra Westfall. Thank you all for teaching me the ins and outs of making memorable desserts and for allowing me to endlessly experiment on you.

And lastly, I want to give a big shout-out to my cohorts in the test kitchen: Tiffany Vickers-Davis, Adam Hickman, Robin Bashinsky, and Kathleen Phillips. Thank you guys for all of your suggestions that helped my recipes taste better and look prettier and for making every day in the test kitchen feel like a play date.

Published by Oxmoor House, an imprint of Time Inc. Books
1271 Avenue of the Americas, New York, NY 10020

Senior Editors: Rachel Quinlivan West, R.D.; Betty Wong
Project Editor: Emily C. Connolly
Assistant Project Editor: Lacie Pinyan
Senior Designer: Maribeth Jones
Executive Photography Director: Iain Bagwell
Photo Editor: Kellie Lindsey
Photographer: Stephen Devries
Senior Photo Stylist: Mindi Shapiro Levine
Photo Stylist: Missie Neville Crawford
Food Stylists: Marian Cooper Cairns, Nathan Carraba,
    Victoria E. Cox, Margaret Monroe Dickey,
    Catherine Crowell Steele
Test Kitchen Manager: Alyson Moreland Haynes
Recipe Testers: Robin Bashinsky, Adam Hickman,
    Julia Levy, Kathleen Royal Phillips, Karen Rankin
Senior Production Manager: Greg A. Amason
Assistant Production Manager: Diane Rose Keener
Associate Production Manager: Kimberly Marshall
Writer: Dianne Jacob
Copy Editors: Jacqueline Giovanelli, Deri Reed
Proofreader: Dolores Hydock
Indexer: *Marra*thon Production Services
Nutrition Analysis: Jessica Cox, R.D.
Fellows: Laura Arnold, Ali Carruba, Nicole Fisher,
    Loren Lorenzo, Caroline Smith

ISBN-13: 978-0-8487-4451-9
ISBN-10: 0-8487-4451-9
Library of Congress Control Number: 2015944366

Printed in the United States of America

10 9 8 7 6 5 4 3 2 1

First Printing 2015